THE WELL-WATERED LAND

THE WELL-WATERED LAND

The life of a Dartmoor hill farmer

Jez Wilkinson

Foreword by Rob Steemson

BLACKINGSTONE
PUBLISHING

First published 2016
Published by Blackingstone Publishing
2 Steward Cottages Moretonhampstead Devon TQ13 8SD

Reprinted 2018, 2021

Photographs courtesy of the Wilkinson family unless otherwise acknowledged. Every effort has been made to trace the copyright holders of photographs, but in some cases this has proved impossible. The author and publishers apologise for any inconsistencies in this respect. Contemporary photographs by Sue Viccars.

Some of the material published in this book has already appeared in
Dartmoor Magazine www.dartmoormagazine.co.uk

Edited by Sue Viccars, Blackingstone Publishing
Designed by Emily Kingston

British Library Cataloguing in Publication Data
A catalogue record for this book is available from the British Library.

ISBN 978 0 9954986 0 0

Typesetting and origination by Blackingstone Publishing
Printed in Great Britain by Short Run Press Exeter Devon

Front cover Young Jeremy Wilkinson with the newly born filly foal sired by Arabian stallion Rustum Bey from a wild Dartmoor mare, 27 April 1951 PHOTOGRAPH **MIRRORPIX**
*Back cove*r Jez and Rowan at Babeny, 2014 PHOTOGRAPH **CLAIRE TUCKER**

CONTENTS

FOREWORD

THEY SAY THAT INSIDE ALL OF US THERE IS A BOOK waiting to be written, and over the years many different books have documented various elements of Dartmoor's history, wildlife and landscape. For over 5000 years farming has been the main land use on the moor, and this has predominantly created and maintained the area that people like to visit and enjoy today. Presently over 90 percent of the land within the National Park boundary is still used for farming. Most of this area has both open and enclosed moorland where livestock is grazed, and the remainder is smaller fields and woodland.

Jez Wilkinson (like his mother Freda before him) follows a long line of people who have lived and worked in a very rural community and have put pen to paper to share their vast experience and intimate local knowledge. This aptly named book is no exception, and provides a fascinating insight into the daily challenges of growing up and living in the middle of Dartmoor. Jez is proudly the third generation of Wilkinsons who tenanted Babeny Farm at the junction of the East Dart and Wallabrook rivers, dividing the Dartmoor Forest from Spitchwick Manor. He farmed this traditional Dartmoor hill farm for forty years, and the property and surrounding 211 acres of land has been recorded since AD1260 as an ancient tenement.

So why have I been given the honour of writing the Foreword for Jez's book? From Jez's perspective he has known me all my life, and (to quote him) I am a 'local boy made good!' I was lucky enough to grow up in the busy village shop at Poundsgate near the Dart Valley. The land immediately around the property was owned by the wider Wilkinson family, and we had the privilege of being able to access their private land in return for helping out at harvest time, feeding orphan lambs, keeping our eyes open and reporting issues. Our respective parents were later neighbours for many years.

Since 1977 Jez has been (and continues to be) the Foreman of the local Spitchwick Commoners' Association. This role involves overseeing the stocking rate and thriftiness of grazing stock on the common, keeping in close contact with the land owner and reporting land issues, concerns or damage to the

LEFT Stepping-stones across the East Dart, Laughter Hole. When Jez was around three years old he was being led across the ford on his pony, behind his mother Freda. His saddle slipped, and Freda grabbed his leg to stop him falling off. 'But we still went across the river with my head under the water!'

other committee members. As Foreman he was automatically a member of the Dartmoor Commoners' Association, and became an inaugural Quarterman member of the Dartmoor Commoners' Council in 1985. It is in his professional role as farmer, Foreman and Quarterman, and mine as a Sector Ranger and Head Ranger, that we have respected each other and worked in partnership on many Dartmoor issues, concerns and problems over the years.

The essence of Dartmoor lies in its enduring granite landscape, its characters, folklore, wildlife, archaeology, flora and fauna, and people's connectivity with their surroundings. Jez Wilkinson is a true Moorman and captivates all this detail in a very personal and passionate account, which touches on the majority of the vast range of human emotions.

'Once a farmer, always a farmer' is a well-known saying, and Jez has now moved to Poundsgate on to a smaller farm. He continues to have an intimate relationship with Mother Dartmoor, and through this book shares his knowledge and experience with a wider audience. I was delighted to be asked to contribute, and I hope you enjoy reading it.

Rob Steemson, Head Ranger
Dartmoor National Park Authority, July 2016

LAUGHTER HOLE

'I first annoyed the world a thousand feet up in the heart of Dartmoor, in the autumn before the 1947 winter. It was so long ago that not many locals remember the 1947 blizzard....'

IN THE BEGINNING

A FEW NOTES FOR MODERN MAN whose great crime is not that he does not know, but that he does not know that he does not know! How tiny is our lifetime's accumulation of knowledge!

I first annoyed the world a thousand feet up in the heart of Dartmoor, in the autumn before the 1947 winter. It was so long ago that not many locals remember the 1947 blizzard. (Not that there are many locals left to remember, as most of Dartmoor is now inhabited by incomers; and if truth were told I don't remember much of it myself as, by necessity, I was breast-fed for the first year of my life, keeping my nose warm you might say.)

That winter, the men of the local village had to take a horse and 'wain' to Princetown, all of six miles across the moor, for supplies of bread, salt, oil for lamps, accumulators for the wireless and so on. They said that on their return the snow crust was so deep they abandoned the wain and led the horse carrying the provisions over the gates as they couldn't open them. It would have been a hard old slog against bitter wind, in low visibility and a ground blizzard.

The house I was born in rejoiced in the name of Laughter Hole, lying halfway between Dartmeet and Bellever on the west bank of the East Dart river. We

Laughter Hole Farm in the 1950s; the young trees of Bellever Plantation (planted just after the Second World War) can be seen in the background. Jez's father Clarence ploughed the wet land of Soussons and Fernworthy prior to Forestry Commission planting

Jez's parents: Clarence (forestry worker and farm labourer) aged twenty-six,
and Freda (originally from London) aged twenty-three

were a mile from the nearest neighbours and, as I was an only child, the old river was friend, playmate and constant companion to me. Although I have moved a little, the Dart and its tributaries were a ribbon stitching my life together through those early years, chattering happily on still June days, adorned with damselflies and kingcups, or in angry spate with lashing rain in winter. They say the Dart claims a life a year, and it got rather close to claiming mine on several occasions. One of my earliest memories was crawling on a small patch of lawn and looking up at towering multi-coloured lupins with daisies all around, so I guess that it must have been early summer. The old folks used to say: 'Don't turn your stock out until you can cover five daisies with your foot.' They had a lot of old stories in those days; perhaps the condition of your stock depended on the size of your feet.

I suppose in a way I was destined to be a bastard of two societies, my father being a forestry worker and farm labourer, and later a smallholder, and my mother having 'come out' in London society then joining the Land Army in the West Country to help with the war effort. She ended up at Lizwell in the parish of Widecombe. My father used to ride from Babeny over Corndon Tor to Lizwell to do his courting once or twice a week, weather and Grandfather permitting!

The world of my infancy was filled with dogs, ponies and gigantic larger-than-life characters: men like Joe Whiteway who used to extract timber from the steep rides and rack-ways in Bellever Forest with an old mare called Blossom. Blossom had wonderful whiskers and on frosty mornings they used to turn to icicles along with her eyelashes. Wages in those days for a man and horse were twelve shillings [60p] a day plus horse allowance. As I sit here now, barely two miles and half a century away, I can still see that old mare and Joe with wisps of mist caressing the leaders of the Douglas fir trees, struggling, sweating and sometimes slipping to their knees, dragging timber up to

Jez with his mother Freda at Laughter Hole in the summer of 1949

Left: Fred Pearce, Jez's maternal grandfather, in the First World War
Right: 'Granny Pearce' and her daughter Barbara (sister to Lyndall and Freda) in about 1912

the roadside. Joe was also the local rabbit trapper, the tools of his second trade being snares and gins (legal in those days). He was a taciturn old blighter, not holding much with nosy precocious boys, although he did once give me two rabbits to take home – and a good stew they made with some swede and teddies. Food was not plentiful in the fifties with rationing and so on, and Father earning the princely sum of three pounds seven shillings and sixpence a week.

Looking back to what is now the first half of the last century it was a harder but simpler world, with more sweat, violence and financial hardships, but perhaps a greater dignity and knowledge of one's place in the overall scheme of things. And mine was a very small and quiet place, partly from respect and partly from self-preservation.

There came a time – as there does in the lives of all small scabby-kneed boys – when I was informed that the great journey of education awaited me in far-off Princetown. I was not in the least impressed and did not see the point, especially if it meant leaving my river, my woods and my spaniel, Puffin, whose enquiring nose and over-vigorous tail escorted my every adventure.

In those days, the school bus was in fact an old van and didn't, or couldn't, make it past Bellever, about a mile away down the forest road. So I borrowed a small Shetland pony and rode him to Bellever every school morning, turning him loose in Mrs Bray's field. I hid the bridle and sack under the hedge and went on to school in the car or van, reversing the procedure in the evening.

From the very first day, school and I did not agree. I found it difficult after five years or so in a thousand-acre wood to adjust to a large number of argumentative, noisy, snotty and devious contemporaries. I blubbed regularly for the first week and irregularly thereafter. Eventually (and after much derision from my schoolmates, who were all lucky enough to know each other) I settled down and came to terms with the three Rs under the stern eye of Mrs Cundit and her ruler, which was used more for rapping knuckles than measurement. But all the knuckle rapping in the world could not improve my spelling, an affliction I have suffered with all my days. Now, in later life, I discover I am slightly dyslexic, although in those days the term was 'slow' or 'lazy'. It was a label I wore with absolute belief.

Eventually there came a time when I considered school had nothing left to teach me. And being a mature lad of seven or eight summers, and with obviously nothing more to learn, my interest was taken with more exciting pastimes and people of the period.

One such character I swiftly adopted as mentor and a second father, partly because my own father was busy and had less time to spare, and partly because of the fascinating aroma of the former's old Derby tweed coat and the inside of his trilby hat.

Peter was semi-retired when he first strolled into my life, having downsized to a smallholding in Sherrill. Although he was born in the latter end of the nineteenth century when schooling was a short and often painful process that interfered with the necessity of existence, he possessed an intensely enquiring mind and a range of skills and practical knowledge that earned him the respect and admiration of his peers for miles around. Peter was never a Jack of all trades, but a master of all the skills required to exist in his time. He was a thatcher, both house and rick, pig killer, butcher, veterinary (before they were invented), knife grinder, water diviner, stonemason and, sitting in front of his peat and turf fire, the teller of wonderful protracted lies, enough to cement him as the hero of any small boy.

Peter didn't smell, as we would describe it in modern times (as in BO), but by all of the laws of nature he should have done. Ruby, his lifetime partner (and incidentally his first cousin), used to rub him down with goose fat in the autumn before he donned his combinations and he stayed in them until spring, only unbuttoning the twin flaps when necessary. I never noticed him having a pulled muscle or arthritis (the screws as we knew it), and he lived to ninety-two, mostly on pure cholesterol and

Peter Hannaford photographed in 1977: 'a man at home in his environment'

cider, as did his father before him to ninety-six. They breakfasted on fat bacon, fresh eggs, clotted cream and cider, and smoked digger shag. And if I remember, his father was said to chew plug tobacco.

Peter's father, although before my time, was a somewhat eccentric individual. Having been thwarted in love as a very young man, he put a 12-bore under his chin, and tilting his head back – presumably for convenience rather than to get a view of his maker – blasted his bottom jaw through the kitchen ceiling. He lived the rest of his noteworthy life with a leather mask covering the lower half of his face and fed from a jug. This arrangement was much to the consternation of the aforementioned Joe Whiteway, among others, who had once been instructed as a youth to take a jug of cider to Mr Hannaford, at that time thatching a rick. Joe took the cider halfway up the ladder and called to Mr Hannaford, who turned to accept the cider. Whereupon Joe, looking up under the mask, promptly passed out, smashing the jug of cider in the process.

SACRIFICE OF THE PIG

Peter, as a representative of an older and more self-sufficient generation, was usually part and parcel of most of the seasonal chores on our post-war smallholding. For a small boy, probably the greatest and most looked forward to day of the year, apart from birthdays and Christmas, was pig-killing day. All the local holdings kept a pig, born probably in May or June and fed on household scraps and a little barley meal and skimmed milk through the summer, and when fat was killed usually just before Christmas. Each holding would kill on a different week and exchange fresh pork joints before salting. In this way we all had fresh pork for maybe a month in early winter.

In our area, we killed on a form or bench, turning piggy upside down, sticking him and holding him until he bled properly, which was important for the quality of the meat. It was quite a task, even for experienced men, when some of the fat pigs weighed in at between twenty and thirty score deadweight, a score being twenty pounds as we measured in those days. I believe in North Devon they used to kill standing with a slip rope around their tushes, entering the knife halfway down the neck and aiming for the root of the tail, just letting the point of the knife drop to sever the main artery that crosses in front of and between the shoulder blades.

To today's generation it must sound barbaric to rear and nurture a pig, make a friend out of it, tickle its tummy, scratch its ears and then slaughter it. But those were different and harder times and the pig was given the leading role in what was a sacrifice to the survival of the household through the dark winter months. There was no concept of cruelty as we would imagine it today. It was just part of the annual routine, and if I was lucky I got the bladder to blow up for a football. In later years, I helped Peter kill his last pig. He was over ninety, and I am sitting looking at the photo as I write.

The way animals were treated in those days is very difficult to explain. Perhaps the old saying that 'a cat is your master, a dog is your servant and a pig is your equal' sums it up to a degree. In the holistic view of life, animals were not treated with deliberate unkindness but were part of the pattern of survival. Without this equal coexistence in the scheme of things, life, both theirs and ours, would have had little chance or meaning.

Perhaps the greater thrill was when Father and I went to return the favour and help Peter and Ruby with their pig. One year stands out in my mind as if it were yesterday. I had been sleeping 'one eye at a time', determined not to miss any part of the great day. I must have been about seven or eight years old. I sneaked out of bed, dark and early, and set about my chores, feeding calves with chopped swede and filling the cows' hay racks from the tallet. Then I did a thousand pumps on the old cast iron pump that lifted the water up from the well to the tank in the house loft; this would just about last the day. It was a job I hated! It made my back ache and blistered my hands, but that day I set to work with a will and had it all finished before Father appeared with a good gash on his chin from the old cut-throat razor he always used and sharpened on a leather strop that he kept behind the kitchen door. The strop also doubled as an article of correction when I misbehaved.

At last all was ready. We walked down through the woods heading for the next valley, where Peter and Ruby lived. The pine trees were sighing and nodding recognition, the pigeons clappering and playing with the wind. It was a middling distance to walk, hard on the feet but easy on an expectant young mind trudging behind Father in the grey Dartmoor dawn, watching the occasional spark fly when his hobnailed boot clipped a stone. Father was a quiet man with little or no conversation, who kept his head down; even so, he noticed more that went on around him than many a man with head in air and too much talk. He never saw the point of emptying his mouth to fill another man's (or his pocket for that matter).

At long last we arrived at Higher Sherrill, Peter's holding, to be greeted by Ben, the old half cattle dog, the other half having been left to Providence and a dark night – that particular pedigree being shared with a few of his two-legged neighbours.

Peter emerged with his old greasy trilby and an apron made from half a West of England hessian sack, much bloodstained. The other half was tied in a neat bundle

Ruby French, 1950. Originally from Holne, Ruby was Peter Hannaford's cousin, but the two lived together as man and wife for many years

containing two killing knives, a steel for sharpening and a hammer with a crook for pulling the claws off the trotters, a saw and a scraper for scraping the bristles when the pig was scalded – the scraper being a much-used sheep's bell which fitted the hand nicely. He also brought a gamber, which was a piece of carved ash about a yard long with nail holes that fitted through the Achilles tendons of the hind legs, with a strong rope to hang the pig up to the stout oak beam that ran across the cart linhay. The wain, or small two-wheeled cart, had been evacuated for the day.

Inside the house Ruby was well prepared with two large black kettles hung on the chimney crooks over the peat fire in the centre of a black cavernous fireplace, and the peat augmented for the special day with some firewood for extra heat. As it was a big pig, some twenty-two score, there was also a large heavy cast iron cauldron with a galvanised lid to stop chimney soot falling in. The fire was drawing well, aided by a strip of oilcloth attached to the chimneybreast; all the water containers were simmering comfortably, ready to render up their contents for scalding in time-honoured fashion, as they had done for generations. The normally cold and draughty kitchen was warmer and more welcoming than I had ever remembered it. A hogshead of cider stood on a trestle in a dark corner. The doorway to the court was shared by a nervous ginger kitten with eyes like golden half sovereigns and a scraggy old Maran hen with her petticoats badly torn and a flat head, obviously suffering from an excess of recent sexual activity.

Centre stage stood Ruby, magnificent in the domination of her realm, wearing a black beret, brown dealer's dustcoat and short wellies with her sturdy calves overflowing above. Men had their place in the scheme of things but here her word was law – and woe betide anyone foolhardy enough to contradict or flout it.

When Ruby gave the word that all was ready we three 'men', armed with two slip ropes, the pig form and a Sheffield eye-witness rivet-handled knife sharp enough to shave with, wandered conversationally down to the pig's house, with me puffing myself up to twice my size in the proud realisation that I was considered old enough to be both witness and water carrier. The two men entered the pig house with a slip rope each, one for the top jaw and one for the back leg, the only two places that you can hamper a pig with any reasonable chance of success. Before disappearing, Peter leans over conspiratorially and whispers to me to be sure and grab the pig by the tail when it emerges. By and by, out comes piggy. I make a rush for a non-existent tail (it had been bitten off at birth by the sow) and went sprawling in the muck, deflating my ego considerably, while those two silly buggers fell about laughing so hard they nearly lost the pig.

Once pronounced properly dead and bled, my job was to carry the large black kettles of boiling water from the fire to the pig form in the cobbled courtyard while Peter and Father scalded and scraped the pig, removing all the bristles with the mandatory peck of dirt (along with the occasional elastic drip that had landed from the end of Peter's nose!). A running commentary was required from me to Ruby as to the area of pig left to scrape and her reserves of boiling water. Once the scraping had been completed to Peter's satisfaction and the hind legs had been spread with the gamber using a stout rope, the pig was hauled up to the main beam. It was now left to set for a short time while we repaired to the hogshead of cider in the kitchen and the dogs and poultry did their best to clear up the steaming and aromatic mixture of hot bristles and congealed blood.

From here on the day took on a more relaxed tone. The pig had been agreeable enough to die well and the cider was having a mellowing influence on all concerned – so much so that Peter embarked on a tale of a notable neighbour who got so drunk that when sawing down the backbone he ended up with both ears on one half, much to the delight of his helpers.

The next job, before cutting down, was paunching or disembowelling. Clean plates were laid out for liver and kidneys, heart, lights, lungs and the rest, and an old tin bath for the intestines. Ruby would later wash and clean them in the stream, ready to fill for black pudding, sausages and so on. In those days people prided themselves on wasting nothing and using everything in a pig 'apart from the squeal'. I can still see the old couple, secure in and unassumingly proud of their skill and labour, performing one of the annual rituals that they had learned from parents and grandparents and which had served them well for decades.

After the pork was jointed and left on the cold slate slabs of the back kitchen or 'pantry', the hams and flitches were salted. Sometimes this was done in a half hogshead of brine, but more often they were dry salted with a pinch of saltpetre and sometimes alum added to the salt. They were thoroughly rubbed with the mixture and turned every day for maybe a week or ten days until they had stopped sweating. They were then placed in muslin and occasionally hung to smoke in the chimney, but more often hung on the meat hooks in the ceiling. There they would stay all winter unless taken down for a slice or two for breakfast or supper.

All the holdings 'pitted and caved' their swedes and potatoes for the winter in shallow trenches. These were about four or five feet wide and ten to twelve feet long, perhaps a foot or eighteen inches deep, earthed over with a Devon shovel and thatched with turf. If properly made, the contents would keep for the winter ready for human consumption, or for sheep and cattle. These 'caves' were a wonderful haven for long-tailed field mice, voles and shrews, and when we opened them in the spring or winter I had a great time with the dogs chasing the vermin. One day taking a wild swing with the shovel and narrowly missing the dog, I barked Father's shins and had to retire from the field of battle in some haste.

Ruby's (or Miss French as I was instructed to call her in the days of childhood) area of expertise and some pride was milking the four or five cows and scalding the milk for cream or butter. In the early days, she used to scald the milk in white enamelled pans floating in larger containers of hot water, the cream rising to the top as a beautiful yellow crust. In latter days she had a cream separator turned by hand. The skimmed milk then went into a bucket to feed the calves. A diet that was exclusively of milk, they used to say, would fat a pig, starve a dog or keep a man alive. Not something I tried. In those days my diet was omnivorous, uninteresting and unhygienic, consisting of almost anything that I could stick in my mouth that wasn't actually poisonous. Sweets were seldom seen, definitely an unaffordable luxury, but the diet was varied and, apart from tea, salt, sugar and paraffin for lamps and primus stoves, most of the holdings were practically self-sufficient. As well as potatoes and swedes, they salted quantities of runner beans and made jams and preserves from a mixture of fruit and swede. We bought bread, but it was of poor quality and used to give the dogs fits if added to their meat.

FIRE – THE LIFE FORCE

In the long winter months, the fire was the heart of the house. It was an ever-present comfort of smouldering vags and wood, changing its moods with the wind direction; sometimes smoking and sulking so badly that you couldn't see the opposite kitchen wall through streaming eyes, and occasionally taking on the bright cheerful crackling personality that welcomed the drying of socks, gaiters, britches, dogs or anything that could find a place between it and the high back settles that we sat in to keep the multiple and vigorous draught from our backs. Summer in front, winter behind, as you might say.

The fire was just another animal to feed and nurture. When well fed it grew fat and healthy and when starved it withered and died; but since prehistory it has been our constant companion or servant, and occasionally enemy, in much the same way as the other wild or domesticated creatures that shared our life, space and time. To gaze deeply into the belly of a fire as we have done for a thousand generations takes stress and fear of the dark unknown and replaces it with an energy and life force that gives a little lift to the tired, the old and the sick, whose own life heat is waning. They say that fire warms you three times: once for cutting, once for carting and splitting and once for sitting and spitting, but they forgot the fourth. It warms your soul when in good company.

Food for the fire was a mixture of vags, turf and wood gleaned from the common. Most of the commoners had rights of estover and turbary that enabled them to gather wood from the common, up to six inches in diameter, which served the dual purpose of keeping the common from getting overgrown and heating the house. Many of these old rights are now seldom used, but must be exercised and protected with vigour. We all remember the old adage that 'To steal a goose from common is a crime. But the greater crime is to steal the common from the goose.'

Kindling or lighting sticks were normally called 'black firing'. They were the burnt sticks left from the last year's swaling. Faggots of ash wood were also used to pack into the furze or bread ovens: bundled and bound, they were the tops from laying hedges. After the faggots were burned out the inside of the oven was then raked out and the baking placed on the hot stone. These ovens were commonly built into the side of the local Dartmoor fireplaces and were made on a heavy granite base that would hold the heat. Most of them had heavy iron doors.

Peter Hannaford and Ruby French with 'one of the last peat fires on Dartmoor'
(traditional in Dartmoor longhouses in those days)

Turf and peat, on the other hand, were slow burning and primarily used on the open fire. This fire Ruby also used for cooking and on Sundays it produced a fine roast. First a baking ring was placed on the hearth, perhaps a foot in diameter, maybe a little more, and was filled with hot ashes. Then the roast, accompanied by the usual teddies, parsnips and so on, was placed on top in a roasting pan. Then the baking kettle as it was called, in likeness to an upside-down cauldron, was placed over the top, being careful not to drop soot into the cooking, and the whole thing was covered or banked over with burning turf. Occasionally I was allowed to help under supervision. The whole operation started at about eight to half past in the morning and was ready to lift, beautifully cooked, at 1pm, although the savoury smells had my mouth watering long before that.

FIRESIDE TALES

As I have said, it was little I thought of school in those days or yet of any relevance it might have for my future life. I wanted only to be a farmer and thought of nothing much else. Any education that filtered through was fireside learning, my schoolroom the old black kitchen, my tutors the disembodied voices of old men rich with the fatigue of experience issuing from dark corners of a passing world. Night after night I remember the firelight flickering on the black grimy fingernails, the horny hands and fingers bent with arthritis, the odd spark of a hob nail on granite, just as if it were yesterday. These were men who as a child I thought as old as Methuselah and yet a moment before they had been young and thrusting entrepreneurs, ambitious, aggressive, vigorous, life's juices hot upon their hand and fire in their bellies.

So I sat and learned, never bored, never tired, but comfortably in awe of the wisdom and the life experience that came from those stubbled old faces, the wisdom born of a shrewd cunning that had brought them through two world wars and the deprivation of the depression in the 1930s. It is strange that to take a coin from a man labels you a thief, but that same man will willingly give you the benefit of a lifetime's hard-won experience, a far greater prize, just for the compliment of listening. The benefit, value and honour of accepting this gift to a child is incredible, a priceless asset if we could but see it through the fog of childhood cares and fancies. But no one ever could put old head on young shoulders.

The hard frosts of midwinter were always likely to prompt one of Peter's favourite tales. The intro was always the same, and always brought the thrill of expectation to me as the old man took out his baccy pouch and carefully packed his pipe with a grubby finger. Leaning over and taking up a glowing turf or red ember from the fire, he would wait until his pipe was drawing to satisfaction, fix me with one eye and – after a long contemplative silence designed to sharpen my anticipation to near breaking point – would start as he always did with, 'Did I ever tell 'bout the day I shot all they snipes?'

'No, Mr Hannaford!' came the inevitable and anticipated lie.

'Well, boy,' as he settled himself and eased his bits, 'you'm 'andy with a shot iron, but back around the turn of the years when old Victoria was still with us we had a brave-ish hard winter, the ground was freezed like a stone, been like it for weeks, not much snow just hard frost, birds was hunger tame, a lot died frozen to the ground, we didn't have a lot to spare either. Well, one morning I looks up thicky old reave and there was just a bitty trickle of water coming down beside the ice, and where the water made the ground soft there was dozens of snipes feeding and hopping about, like bloody sparrows they woz.

'Well, not to miss the chance of a feed I slipped in and fetched Father's old muzzleloader, poured in a good measure of powder from the flask, but when I went for the shot the pouch was empty. Well, I wasn't going to be beat so I rammed down a good wad with the ramrod, then took out the rod, sharpening the small end to a good point and putting it back in the gun, back I goes to the bottom of the reave. All they snipes was still there feeding plus a few more that came along for the company. I crockied down, quiet like, took good aim and let drive up the reave, bang!' Peter would always pause at this juncture to bring out the full flavour of the scene. 'When I laid down the iron and walked up through the smoke, I picked up thicky ramrod and it had forty-nine snipes on un.'

Now came my part in the production. 'Mr Hannaford,' says I, trying not to giggle, 'why didn't you make it fifty?' Peter would carefully knock out his pipe on the granite fireplace, fix me with an eye loaded with disappointment, lean over and whisper, 'Boy, you don't believe I should tell you a damned lie over one little old snipe do you?'

The magic never waned and the fire never seemed to go out.

WINTER MILKING

Early morning milking was one of my favourite jobs. Father and I would venture across the dark and usually wet farmyard on cold winter mornings with a galvanised bucket each and an old hurricane oil lantern. We would hang the lantern on a convenient nail and throw six or seven swedes into the trough of each of the fifteen or so milking cows, along with two or three wads of hay down into the racks from the tallet above. When the winter mornings were dark, windy and bitterly cold – as they usually were – the shippon was a wonderful microclimate. With the warm glow of the oil lamp the tiny clouds of moist breath from the cows' nostrils would turn to droplets on their eyelashes while they chewed their cuds.

Each one, chained in pecking order and glad of the warmth and the companionship, would rise hind end first and in her turn cheerfully submit to pail, three-legged milking stool and warm hands. Depending on each individual character, after one or two minutes the cows would let their milk down to experienced hands in long jets steaming into the bucket, maybe two or two-and-a-half gallons of sweet warm milk with perhaps two or three inches' head of froth, depending on the strength and experience of the milker's wrist. Father always out-milked me while pretending not to be competitive and I was straining every sinew. The swedes had to be carefully topped as the cows would grab a mouthful of top and shake vigorously, sending the bulb of the swede – which was perhaps one or two pounds in weight – whizzing across the shippon, occasionally with dire consequences.

I still remember, as old long-dead friends, Judy, Jonquil, Janet, Aster, Alice and Alison, each family line starting with the same initial.

CUTTING PEAT

In those days a good percentage of the turf and peat was harvested locally. When there was a good break in the weather between the other seasonal work, come June time, those locals that still clung to the old ways would sharpen up the old turf irons which were made from a wide heavy handle with a steel blade shaped roughly like a heart, the whole thing four feet high. The women would pack jugs of rough cider and bottles of cold tea, bread and cheese and so on for the day. When the men were sweating hard in mid-June's sun, cold tea was a refreshing drink, while cider helped with the backache and numbed the over-active mind. It was, as I remember, a very effective laxative for those of us young and stupid enough not to know when we had had too much, but what matter when high on the heath with none but the skylarks, plover and curlew for an audience (and a good handful of sphagnum moss for a wipe).

The curlew, one of my favourite birds, has disappeared from our high moorland now along with the peewit or plover, although we still have some golden plover.

But back to business. After a hot trek up to the tops of Riddon Ridge or Yar Tor the men would find a suitable area with a good vein of peat under, stash their waistcoats, cider, tea and the rest and find a suitable tree to hang the grub against the dogs. And then to work, taking off the top layer of turf.

Being young I was known, to my secret annoyance, as the 'hobbledy-hoy', neither man nor boy, and as the child I had to work with the women, stooking the turf or vags, much like you would stook sheaves of corn after the binder had cut and tied them. This kept all but the ends off the damp ground and let the air circulate to dry them if the weather held. If there was a nice cooling breeze it filled up my eyes with peat dust which also found its way into every wrinkle and crevice, creating a black soup which ran in small rivulets from my collar downwards, leaving sticky tide marks.

When the cooling breeze stopped I was attacked by the grey flies with feathery feet and sharp noses, bringing up itchy lumps and weals on any bare skin they could find. The older and wiser generation never exposed their skin to either sun or insects, and for the men a straw hat was probably the only concession to hot summer days, with long-sleeved shirts rolled up to just below the elbow. Although my mother and aunt were modern enough to wear slacks with a zip placed very properly at the side of the hip, the older ladies had summer frocks, sometimes with petticoat and bloomers. Any insect venturing within was sure of an uninteresting and puzzling time.

The work was hard, and to a small hobbledy-hoy the hot June day seemed to go on forever, broken only by three meal breaks. Crib was usually a sandwich with cheese or clotted cream and lemonade made with powder, sweet and still, much nicer than the gassy rubbish of modern supermarkets. How I enjoyed the break with a glass

Peter Hannaford cutting peat on Yar Tor

in one hand, sandwich in the other and perhaps a kestrel sitting on the wind above us with patches of cloud and sunlight playing tag across the patchwork of fields, leaving the moor all the way to the far-off sea at Torbay. Skylarks would spring from the rough molinia grass or 'flying bent' with their delicate and beautiful song that lands so sweetly on the human ear, and yet reverberates with territorial violence and jealousy. Dinner strictly at one was usually a 'teddy oggie', or a piece of rabbit pie with bread and salty homemade butter washed down with cold tea. We always went home at teatime for bread and cream with jam, or 'thunder and lightning' as we called it which was bread and clotted cream with Lyle's golden syrup or treacle on top. The treacle tin bore a small picture of a presumably dead lion and with a swarm of flies or bees, with the motto 'Out of the strong came forth sweetness'. I could never work out what the hell a swarm of bees would want with a dead lion but never dared ask for fear of looking stupid.

At tea and dinner, Father as the head of the family would sit in the old carver at the top of the table, the other men came next and then the women, and as the only child I sat at the bottom. After the tea had been allowed to 'draw' it was poured out in strict order. The men would always tip tea from the cup into the saucer to cool it. I think Mother felt this was not quite the thing, but it was traditional with the labouring men and often, as the men drank from their saucers, the slurping would drown the conversation.

MIDSUMMER WHEELS

At around the same time as we had the satisfaction of seeing all the turf spread out to dry, the thoughts of the parish, especially the youth of the parish, turned to midsummer amusement. On midsummer night most of the locals turned out of their armchairs and settles, and made their way to Meltor Corner overlooking the Dart on Dr Blackall's Drive. Any transport was commandeered to take provisions, which were mostly of the liquid variety, and also several cart or wain wheels. The view down the steep furze-clad sides of the valley, looking perhaps a quarter of a mile straight down to Mother Dart, twinkling like a tiny diamond bracelet in the cushion of the oak woods was, and is, breathtaking.

Usually an informal committee was formed of Frenches, Caunters, Nosworthys, Coakers and anyone else sober enough to be of any use. Peter Hannaford was Foreman of the common, an office bestowed upon him by the commoners and freeholders of the parish at the Court Leet, a traditional meeting called by the Lord of the Manor, then Mr Simpson, and the commoners from time to time to iron out any communal problems,

(Left to right) Jasper French, Stan French and Jack Nosworthy outside the Tavistock Inn, Poundsgate, 1950s – 'three of the best-known locals in the area'. Jack Nosworthy lost an arm in France during the First World War

and the Foreman had the last word. The cartwheels were bound with twisted straw ropes and soaked in tar, and when Peter had picked the right spot for the longest clear run, they were fired and rolled. As they picked up speed and the wind fanned the flames they made a glorious and exciting sight, racing and bouncing towards the river far below. Wagers were often taken on the distance each wheel would roll before it broke up in a shower of golden sparks, exploding into the soft velvet summer night. The wagers could end in arguments or even fisticuffs depending on the amount of

cider taken. But when as a small boy I 'showed fright' at the strong language and temporary aggression, I was quickly counselled: 'Don't 'ee worry, chiel. More bones was made under Meltor than was ever broke', which not only amused and consoled me but gave me the idea that I could look forward to getting a 'fern ticket' of my own.

SINGLING TURNIPS

Around the summer solstice, along with the turfing came a legion of other worries, governed mainly by the weather and family health, although I never noticed anyone have time off to be sick or indisposed. Singling turnips, tail-locking sheep, weeding turnips and swedes, shearing sheep, mowing grass, turning and baling, in the early years occasionally making ricks, either loose or bales, cutting meadow rushes with a scythe to thatch the ricks – one job followed another in steady monotony through the long summer months, with only the occasional fishing trip down to the Dart with a worm, or perhaps a show at the village fête to break the tedium.

Turnips were the main crop apart from grass, drilled in lines up through the field with an old machine that kept within its bowels a perplexing series of cogwheels, springs and tiny cups that picked up three or thirteen seeds at a time and sent them down a spring chute which muzzled them into the soil at about half an inch depth and thick as fleas on a fuzzpig's back. As they grew they had to be singled early, leaving one plant to about four inches before they matured into a tangled, perverse and character-building line. I think I hated the man who had invented that turnip drill.

The singling was usually a family affair. Sometimes a neighbour could spare some time to help at the weekends, but usually the team was Father in the first row, then Auntie Dorothy followed by me, and Mother bringing up the rear. Singling four rows at a time we could soon make quite a respectable patch in a five-acre field. After a few days my hands, not being as tough and calloused as the adults', used to blister and Granny Wilkinson supplied sticking plaster along with powdered lemonade and sweet tea. In those days the term 'child labour' hadn't been invented. All the youngsters in the farming families strove to join in and help with the routine adult tasks. They felt sidelined and rather small if not allowed to take on some of the more arduous or sometimes slightly dangerous tasks usually connected with the larger livestock. We each had our own hoe, not unlike the garden hoes of today but much sharper. We ragged them regularly with the carborundum stone to keep the cutting edge bright and sharp. Backache, blisters and sore dusty feet lengthened the days spent hoeing. Cheerful banter, lemonade and the feeling of growing up and being useful served to shorten them.

Although the working days were hot and dusty in the summer months, with early mornings and late evenings, the still starlit nights were always a joy to me, especially up on the high moor. To lie in the springy heather damp with dew, the only soul for miles watching the stars die one by one and listening to the snipe drumming overhead with the wild strange cry of the curlew or the peewits as they lapped the wind or struggled along in front of you with a broken wing, trying to lead you away from their nests occupied by tiny puffs of chicks. Perhaps to spend a lifetime or even a few stolen hours high on the close-cropped turf under a big sky is about as close as some of us non-believers can ever get to the wonder of a world that, like a heavy cloud, can sometimes for the lucky few roll back to reveal a breathtaking sunset or the occasional questing ray of a half-formed faith.

MY BIRTH TREE

As I grew through those early years and started putting down roots in my native soil, I gradually became aware of an unorthodox companion in my life. It would seem that two cousins of mine in the next village had thought it a fine idea when I was born to plant a rowan tree for me, a tree that would grow with me and listen to the many grievances that are always on a child's mind. Sometimes on windy days she would move under my hand and, bowing her head gently, whisper to me. We have known each other for many years. She is always cheerful and a source of comfort when sad times or unpleasant duties crowd the mind, unlike the sombre pines that stand in regiments, darkly proud, and sigh disapprovingly at the breeze.

The older folks used to call the rowan the witches' tree or quick-beam. It was said to have magical qualities. In those days there were several local witches, most of them white, and they would cure warts, ringworm and suchlike. Provided you followed their instructions to the letter you were sure of a cure. A great many traditional jobs and pastimes were run on superstition and folklore. The harvest was of course the most important time of the year, but even at harvest time it was said that if you saw a light yellow frog it was sure to be fine weather coming, or if it was a dark green one that meant wet weather and the cutting date would be adjusted accordingly.

The old girls would beat a toad or a fuzzpig to death with a stick. Ruby called the fuzzpigs 'cow suckers' and killed them at every opportunity. How she imagined a small insectivore with a tiny mouth full of little needle teeth could suck the large teats of a recumbent cow, or even why the cow would let it, is beyond common sense or reason. I can only imagine that if the cows were newly calved and in the first flush of milk, when they lay down the milk would dribble onto the pasture and the fuzzpig, ever the opportunist, was occasionally seen licking the milk from the grass. This would obviously lead to a hostile reaction from the farmer's wife, as milk, butter, cream and eggs were her department and her source of pin money. On market days Ruby would harness up the old pony and trap and jog off to Newton Abbot to sell her wares and buy essentials, a round trip of perhaps thirty miles or so.

A large part of country life was governed by these superstitions. Some of it was common sense; mostly it was to do with the weather, or what Grandma was remembered to have said when having a hot flush. A few of the old sayings I have found over many years to be true. For example, if the weather changes on the last quarter of the moon, eight times out of ten it will not change again for at least a month. Often, in an exceptionally dry summer, a high wind will break dry springs quicker than rain – and if after a long period of rain and wind when the springs eventually break, the weather will shortly turn back to dry. But other superstitions, like not bringing redcurrant into the house, seemed to have little base (apart from perhaps the scent). It was of course considered very bad luck to cut alder and Granny once told me this was because the cross of Jesus was made of alder. Not being familiar with the timber of the Middle East, and I was left to guess at its authenticity.

SHEEP SHEARING

After the turnips were finished, the first few dry days would see Father put a snaffle bridle on old Henry the black cob, throw a West of England hessian sack over his back, whistle up Patsy Fagin, the Welsh border collie (named after the vicar of

Kingskerswell, presumably, God only knows why) and ride out over the high moor. He was often accompanied by Mother, although that combination usually ended up in strife and hard words, bringing the sheep in for shearing, with Patsy Fagin perhaps working half a mile away on the next tor. It was beautiful to watch the long lines of sheep picking their way down through the valleys like the spokes of some giant wheel leading down to the hub at the farm gate, kicking up skylarks and dust in equal quantities with the old Dart chuckling and winking far below.

Some farmers tail-locked in their sheep a few weeks before shearing, but these were lower farms with more grass and shittier sheep. Father and I had previously made pens of hurdles around the old threshing barn that we used as a shearing shed. On seeing the pens, the older and more experienced ewes that knew the game

Algie May and Marion Howard (on horses by Freda's stallion Rustum Bey)
driving sheep home from Corndon Tor in summer

would often break back at the last minute, to be arrested and cuffed back into line by Patsy and her apprentice child, Ruff.

Shearing was, like many of the jobs in those days, a communal task. Neighbours helped each other in turn, and in those pre-telephone days when few people had motorised transport, the socialising that accompanied any shared activity was greatly looked forward to and took the edge off the labour. Shearing was all done by hand shears, and blessed was the man who could shear with both hands. The women rolled the fleeces into tight bundles ready for the wool packers. The shearers would shear for two hours at a time with ten-minute breaks through the day. Bent double with aching backs and sweat running into their eyes, each sheep was a new challenge.

Each one objected in varying degrees, but the hardship was usually borne with

good humour and occasional ribbing or a joke or two, despite the discomfort and the probability of being tried out for flavour by the sheep ticks and lice that infested the sheep in the days before chemical sheep dips. If the sheep were thin or not in good general condition, the lanolin would not rise away from the skin, making shearing difficult as the shears would not push through the wool with ease. It made the job slow and tempers hot, giving rise to the oldest shearing joke: when the impatient farmer, standing with thumbs in belt and belly hanging over, suggests to the tired shearer that, 'as he was taking so long perhaps the sheep could do with a turnip for sustenance during the operation', it always prompted a swift reply that, 'If the bugger had been given a turnip when she needed it, I would have been finished ten minutes ago, Gov.'

Shearing was for the dogs a complete joy. Swift, busy, responsible, drawing on generations of careful breeding, always trying to out-think the sheep and occasionally us, ever ready with a reproachful eye when a shearer mistakenly let a sheep slip, sulking when laughed at for letting their own sheep escape, most good dogs take their jobs seriously. They definitely do not like to be laughed at and when off-duty they would lie under anything that provided a semblance of shade with tongues lolling in the dirt and a respiration that most vets would deem impossible.

When each pen was finished the sheep were marked with red dye, a mixture of red ochre and sump oil, a patch on the back of the neck and one on the root of the tail. This was Father's mark for identification and well known in our area of the moor. Between minor chores I would watch avidly while the men were shearing, trying to remember each stroke or 'blow' of the shearer's hand and the way the sheep were turned by his feet. Desperate to learn and be of some use, I would practise when the men were at ease or having their crib. My wrists were not strong enough for the springy hand shears at first and the sheep got bored with waiting. Struggling to their feet they bolted off around the shed with me in tow, much to the amusement of the shearers and spoiling the fleeces in the muck. I was soon relegated to sweeping up the 'dag ends' with no argument, as when Father was stressed and tired he always kept his temper within easy reach.

When the sheep were in the pens was also time to castrate and tail the lambs. Peter and Father would sit on each end of a strong board, Father holding the lambs upside down while Peter castrated the ram lambs with a 'burdizzo' or bloodless emasculator (a modern invention for us). The old shepherds used to cut the purse and bite out the testicle – the crunching action of the teeth was said to inhibit the bleeding. The testicle was then spat into a bowl for future use. The tails were cut off with a sharp knife and kept for use in lamb's-tail pie. Not much was wasted. Peter didn't hold with the old ways and, as an interesting and avid conversationalist, a mouthful of lambs' testicles would have inhibited the flow and deprived us of many a good and colourful anecdote.

Those halcyon days and long summers seemed to last for ever within the small window of a child's vision, knowing only the security and protection of hard proud men and kindly thrifty women, little realising that ever at their back stalked the threat of hunger and disgrace that failure would bring. The fear of disease, injury or a bad winter was ever present. As children we were never allowed to share these concerns: they were the concerns of the heads of the families and we were left secure in the knowledge that only very old people got sick, that life as we knew it would go on for ever and that the bluebells and the larks would rise again every spring, and the old River Dart would murmur away below my Rowan tree for, at the very least, a few thousand cuckoo summers. Happy days, self-sufficient days, a life that would label us as peasants (a derisive term in modern times), although we considered ourselves almost middle-class. Perhaps it was only derisive to those who didn't know the qualities it took to be successful in a demanding and very basic way of life.

Jolly Lane Cott: said to have been built in one day

In those days we were perhaps more independent, resourceful, self-supporting and in step with the environment than anyone can boast of being today. As a growing child one of my greatest pleasures was listening to the older men who came to share with us and help us at haymaking, sheep-shearing and gathering livestock from the commons. This was the tradition of mutual support going back for hundreds of years, and such great storytellers they were. In those days nothing much was written down, and the past and present history of local people and their ancestors were all passed on by word of mouth, even such laws and customs as the old right to build a house in a day.

There was one of these houses close to us. It was called Jolly Lane Cott at Hexworthy. Freehold rights could be claimed if a piece of land was enclosed and a dwelling completed on it between sunrise and sunset. They say that in the 1830s, on June Fair day in Ashburton when all the farmers who had rights on the common were away at the fair, the local labourers who had already collected all the materials in readiness, worked together to help one of their number, called Satterley, build a small granite cottage, thatch it and light a fire in the grate by sunset. Although the Duchy of Cornwall tried to charge a small nominal rent, the Satterleys lived there up until the turn of the century.

TALL-TALE TELLERS

In quieter times when the men were resting, old tales of past times would spill from their memories, like the tale of old Dinah Tuckett of Dunnabridge Farm. She was the last of the Duchy pound keepers who regularly took her eggs, cream and other produce to Ashburton in her pony and trap. She was a fat old maid and crabby with it. At Newbridge on the Dart there was at that time a moor gate across the road. Local children manned this gate on market days, opening and shutting it for travellers who tossed them a halfpenny or farthing for their pains. Apparently Dinah was not in favour of this practice, and consequently the children were not much in favour of Dinah. The outcome was that, on reaching the gate, not only did she have to clamber down from the trap but the bit of timber necessary to prop it open had mysteriously disappeared. Dinah soon settled the problem by unhanging the heavy five-barred gate, hitching it to the trap, dragging it to the middle of the bridge and hurling it into the torrent below.

Dinah also used to enter her pony in the Huccaby Tor races. In 1909 the guests of honour were the Prince and Princess of Wales who (according to Freda's notes on the occasion) watched from a little flower-decked glass pavilion set among the rocks and heather. Dinah's nephew was given the 'leg up' but didn't perform to her satisfaction so, oblivious to the royal presence, she thundered down to the course and dealt both jockey and pony a good flying thwack with her blackthorn stick, hollering to the assembled company that 'both the lazy buggers could gallop if they had a mind to'.

Half a century ago, long before the modern distractions of television, computers, DVDs, ipods, blogs and the like, those old purveyors of history, folklore, experience and even the moral discipline born of necessity and shortage, were the idols of a small child with only a tiny window of time and opportunity for homespun education. They were characters who had taken up the same tools and told the same tales as their fifteenth-century forebears, men and women who without word of mouth would have melted unremembered into the medieval mists that still swirl ghostlike around the tors of Dartmoor today. The insidious urban conquest was yet to come.

Another old yarn that was a favourite of Peter's was the tale of Snaily House and the two sisters. I never tired of hearing it, although there was a twist in its tail that I could never quite understand and didn't ring true. But it was a darn good yarn and it seems it has since passed into folklore.

Snaily House was very 'small holding', now in ruins, within a forestry plantation on the bank of the East Dart river on the opposite side of the valley to Laughter where I was born. Originally known as Whiteslade, sometime in the late seventeenth or early eighteenth century it was granted by the Duchy along with the larger acreage on the western bank of the river to the Forestry Commission. In the 1920s Whiteslade or Snaily House had no road leading to it, just half a mile of open moorland between it and Bellever, or an equally rugged path leading southeast to Babeny. The ground is so steep that no wheels have ever been used on it. Nowadays, under the dark trees nearly buried by the decaying spruce needles of half a century, there still lies the ghost of a little farm and remnants of tiny enclosures, carefully terraced, sheepfolds and the ruin of a shippon for about six cattle, with room for a small dung heap. Just above the natural stepping-stones lies the old house built into the hillside, a main room with an open hearth and a little salt cupboard and small windows.

The story was that many years ago the smallholder and his wife died, and the older children had flown the nest leaving only the two younger sisters, who knew no other life and kept themselves to themselves, shy as fox cubs, hiding from anyone who passed or showed any interest in them. They eventually grew too old to swing a scythe and too shy or too proud to ask for help. There was no fodder left to feed the old cow who died chained up in the shippon, there was no food left and the sheep and ponies broke in from the common over the tumbledown gaps and boundary walls and shaved the grass right up to the door. Winter snows drifted in through the great gaps in the thatch, but the two sisters still lived and looked well fed.

Rumours grew among the neighbours that they were witches. How else could they survive? Though they roamed their ruined land and were sometimes seen on the moor beyond, they never went as far as a neighbour's house, to say nothing of a shop. Finally the time came when no one remembered seeing the old girls about for months and, hesitantly, the neighbours decided to go and find out what had happened. The sisters were both found dead in their beds under the rotting thatch and in the house there was no food, only a little salt in the salt cupboard and in the dairy several milk 'steans'. These were the enamelled pans that the cream was scalded in and they were packed with salted down black slugs. These slugs were common on the moor in damp weather and were locally known as snails, real snails as we know them being very uncommon on the high moor.

That was the particular version of the snail's house story as told to me by Peter, who had lived next door to Snaily House or Snails House all his life and, as he carefully explained, he had it from his old neighbour Mrs Annie White who was born a Connybeare from Laughter Hole across the valley, which is probably as good a route as any for a good old Dartmoor yarn. I use the term yarn advisedly as, on reflection, we all know that salt turns slugs into liquid, so perhaps the mouth-watering thought of a regiment of nice fat slugs salted in ready for a hungry winter might contain just a small portion of licence, or even a pinch of salt!

HEAVY HORSE WORK

While still young and wet behind the ears, probably hardly into double figures, I was allowed to work with the horses. Dartmoor was still behind most of the country as regards mechanisation. Grandad Wilkinson, known as 'the boss', still kept a horse or two in the late fifties for the lighter work, pulling a wain or sweeping the loose hay into the rick. The wain as used in our parts was the Cornish wain, a flat-bottomed, two-wheeled cart often with lades (extensions to carry hay), used in place of the wagon which was popular on the bigger farms with flatter land. The wagon had four wheels with a turntable incorporated into the front axle. This turned as a semicircular table in the head of the wagon with shafts attached to the front axle by a pin. The front axle could then be turned almost at right angles to the body of the wagon. Both the wain and the wagon had wooden rollers acting as a windlass at the back to tighten the ropes and to hold the load tight.

Old Peter also had a tip cart, I think it was called a timbrill, for turnips and the like. The tailboard could be removed and a tipstick held the body of the cart down behind the shafts. When this was taken out and the horse backed a step or two the cart would tip, depositing its load on the ground. It was easy to upright it again as the horse moved forward.

As a youngster my first working affair was with those same heavy horses, Blackie and Pleasant. They were honest and gentle without the agenda that comes with the fine-boned Thoroughbreds, dancing and sidling and showing the whites of their eyes, nor yet the lean and limber hunters that I knew so well in later life, scattering stone and turf from hedge banks and cutting up the grass fields with their reckless galloping. The Shire and Clydesdale crosses were power-packed and steadfast, with wise Roman profile heads, muscular crests, wide-bosomed and haunched like Hercules, their silky feathers swinging about their heels as they strode as gallantly as any Highland laird with kilt swinging around his knees.

Too often I collected 'a slice of tongue pie' for not keeping up with the work rate, as I used to be a bit of a dreamer in the time away from the sweaty company and merriment around the rick. I would be sweeping in the strolls and then clean raking the fields all over again, dreaming perhaps of Blackie and Pleasant's relations who, I

Joe Whiteway pulling timber out of Bellever Wood with his horse Blossom

was told, had been picked out by the remount officer to go to war for their country and haul guns and shells in far-off smoking fields. And in all probability to die an unquestioning death from wounds or exhaustion in Flanders mud.

Of course, the book of life is full of pages, each with two sides, and on the other side were the 'red letter' days when the working horses brought home the red, white and blue rosettes from the local shows and prizes from ploughing matches. These were days when they stepped so steady and true to score the straightest furrow in the field, and days when they took the painted wagon to town with Pleasant in the shafts and Blackie as fore horse in tandem: their harness freshly cleaned with black oil, the best hames on their collars and swing brasses on breast plates, loin straps and check reins, all a-glitter and a-jingle with their burnished brass medallions, proud and kind, with somewhere in their ancestry the great show stallion Cornish King Maker or perhaps his progeny.

HAY HARVEST

My very favourite horse work in high summer (although the horses didn't agree on account of the heat and the flies) was sweeping the loose hay into the rick. Father, Mother and Aunt Dorothy would prepare a mattress of thorn and gorse bundles – known as blasts or fuzz fleeces – for the rick to keep the hay off the wet ground. Mother and Dorothy would make the rick, a skilful job for experienced hands, while Father would pitch to the rick with a two-pronged prang. Rewinding half a century

– remembered by the endless sunny days, the scent of fresh meadow hay, daisies and buttercups, the haze of pollen, gentle banter and the satisfaction of a good square rick made against a hard winter – forgotten are the sweat, blisters, harness rubs, biting horseflies and hard words, but I suppose, as they say, 'The further back you plough the years, the better the soil.'

The hay sweep was a long beam of hardwood with stout curved handles at the back and long wooden iron-tipped teeth in front. It was dragged along the strolls of hay by a single horse using double trace chains, each attached to an end of the beam. A load of hay was gathered on top of the teeth and I had to be careful not to let them dig into the ground, or ride up over the hay and leave it behind. When we were fully loaded I could hardly see over the piled loose hay and had to rely on Blackie to navigate back to Father and the rick. On reaching the rick Blackie, knowing the job better than I, would stop and back two or three paces while I hollered for Father to come and help lift the heavy sweep so that the teeth would catch in the ground. Then, as Blackie walked on, the sweep would roll over the load of hay leaving it at the foot of the rick. If he didn't move quickly enough on command, Father was left holding the full weight of the load and ''oss' would collect a broadside of bad language for as long as he stood still.

Some of the best nagsmen, or horsemen, of that time carried with them a small black piece of soft leather or vellum about the size of two fingers. They went to great lengths to obtain these charms. When a mare foals, occasionally the foal is born with this piece of soft material lying on top of its tongue, unattached. It is usually swallowed or rejected, but when found it was carefully dried and kept about the person and when a horse was frightened or skittish, a sniff of the charm (or lackanay) would immediately calm and soothe the animal. The best nagsmen had many old tricks and charms, but perhaps the best trick was a combination of kindness and patience. They lived with their horses as a member of the herd and an equal partner in sweat and labour, often sleeping with the horse in the warm stable in preference to the wife in the bedroom! A good horse would be a friend that worked beside his man for perhaps a third of the man's working life.

Both man and horse often died in the shafts, as it were, both well acquainted with death. Every time they ploughed a furrow together a thousand creatures, no less sentient for being very small, had been torn apart and crushed by the steel ploughshare and coulter, and exposed to the gaping screaming beaks of the seagulls that swooped and flapped, quarrelling behind the plough. Death was the inevitable lot of all that had been given life and the working man was ever on close terms with it.

CHANGING TIMES

Even at leisure, a favourite pastime was rabbiting with ferret and nets. The netted rabbit had little time for fear. A sharp blow behind the ears with the side of the hand and all was over, with a free meal to look forward to. Youngsters of today are caught in a clash of cultures. On the one hand, Mr Disney's anthropomorphism and the teacher's tales of Little Grey Rabbit and so on, and on the other hand, men forged in hard times who knew when killing was necessary and that it must be done quickly and skilfully. I suppose we all hope that our own death will be as merciful, but God is rarely so deft, even after all the practice He has had. Many men of Father's and Grandfather's generation, having seen the passing of two world wars and many hard times, both lived and died with the sort of stoic courage that the better educated and the incomers usually mistook for stolid insensitivity. It was an armour that allowed them to meet all that life could throw at them, a quiet manliness with less complaining than many of the present generation could aspire to.

But alas, even in those careless far-off days of sunny childhood, time and change, those ancient partners were ever snapping at our heels, and Pleasant and Blackie worked themselves quietly and uncomplainingly into eternity, to be replaced eventually by an old, smelly and noisy Fordson tractor, spiteful and uncompromising. It had the ability to plough three times the acreage and pull twice the load, but it would never greet you with the soft muzzle and the throaty chuckle that a horse makes to greet a long-awaited friend. Nor did the tractor have to be taken to the farrier, who was stationary in those days, perhaps ten or twelve miles away at Moorshop, lurking in his warm blacksmith's shop, a centre for all the news and gossip in the area. Apart from knowing all the gossip, Smithy had to know the feet and temperament of every horse, pony and cob in the parish, and often had the shoes ready-made for regular clients. Horses were shod hot and the shoes were made to fit the foot, not the foot made to fit the shoe. The shop had an atmosphere all of its own with the ringing stroke of the hammer on the anvil, the clatter of the newly shod feet on the cobbles, the duller thud of the hammer on the red-hot iron and the hiss of the hot iron in the cooling trough. There was that wonderful acrid smell of scorched hoof and a sulphury smell from the coals that glowed bright in the sooty gloom. The tools of Smithy's trade – the hammers, the pincers, the paring knives and all the paraphernalia that lay in his traditional wooden box – must go back to the beginnings of history, as no doubt did his worn leather apron, split down the middle (and probably also his colourful Anglo-Saxon remarks, when the horse leaned on him or took its foot away).

THE GOLDEN PONY

I suppose at about the double-figure stage of life I was starting to feel my feet, as they say, or at least feel the need of company nearer my own age. The family unit was all very well, but perhaps the next valley might just be a little greener than ours and I was never good at taking Father's word for it. But of course to spread my wings, so to speak, and widen my horizons I needed transport. For a while, I hunted around thinking I could cobble together an old bicycle that Father had abandoned in the stinging nettles, but after discovering that the moving parts were all rusted together and the wheels were different shapes, my eventual salvation came in the form of a pig called Alice.

Alice and Emily were saddlebacked virgin pigs or 'gilts', typical teenagers with attitude, into everything – and if they couldn't eat it or break it they just rolled it in the muck. One day in the early spring, Alice's 'whatever' attitude suddenly changed. She became a different pig, vainly searching the furthest corners of the yard trying to lift the gates off their hinges and so on. Father, having more experience of the facts of life than I, quickly diagnosed a bad attack of love. 'Pig's in season,' says he. 'We will drive her over to Newman Caunter's boar this evening after the yard work is finished.'

We started early as the days were short, me with a bucket of pig food in front making pig-friendly noises and Father behind with a half sheet of galvanised iron and stick to help her on her way. The bucket worked best. You can lead a pig with food, but trying to drive it is a tiresome occupation for both parties. After a while Alice trotted along happily enough, with all the outward signs and body language that accompany the excitement of a dirty weekend. The road was long, white and dusty over Brimpts and Brown Berry to Dunnabridge, but eventually we all arrived to find Mr Caunter well 'in his cups' and Mr Boar well in his mud wallow, but a whiff of Alice's porcine perfume soon emptied the wallow and Mr Boar clambered aboard, mud, grit and all. Piggy sex is a snuffling protracted affair with little or no romance and equipment reminiscent of a carpenter's toolbox. Being slightly embarrassed and bored, I sauntered away out of the yard to look over a hedge into the next field – and across a crowded nettle patch our eyes met!

Blaze was an all-round 'good egg', no malice, no chips on shoulders, and from that first moment we shared genuine mutual interests: youth and a healthy dislike for the regimented responsibility of 'crabbed age'. There was no species prejudice here; this was the brother I never had, a rotund 14.2 hand chestnut with a kind eye, four white feet and a speculative gaze that went right through you and came out the other side, primed with more knowledge than it should have decently acquired. Neither Mr Caunter nor his family rode to any great extent, so perhaps Blaze was surplus to

Young Jez with one of Mrs Tittlemouse's foals (and Flicker the spaniel), 1952

requirements? Unfortunately, money was tight at home and an extra mouth to feed that wasn't bringing in income would have been out of the question.

The road home seemed much shorter with Alice trotting merrily home in front of Father, busting to tell Emily of her adventures, and me legging it behind the pair of them desperately trying to hatch a campaign containing enough logic and careful planning to secure Blaze as my friend and taxi. The thrill of ownership was not so strongly developed at that age, but a permanent friend was something to be carefully requested and, if necessary, fought for. There was, of course, always Puffin. She was a friend but shared as a family pet and I guess dogs, like women, will usually go where they are best fed.

Well, they do say it's better to be born lucky than rich and it so happened that about this time Father managed to get permission from the landlord (the Forestry Commission) to run our cattle out on the spare grazing around Bellever Forest. With no fences to speak of, this involved the cattle wandering over the best part of 2000 acres liberally sprinkled with ditches, bogs, clitters of rocks and most of the cattle traps that Mother Nature could provide! Father was working five-and-a-half days a week for the Commission and had to take care of the cultivation and seasonal work on the holding as well, while Mother dealt with the house cow, pigs, poultry and the rest. 'Man to the plough, woman to the cow' was the old saying. This left no one to herd the outlying cattle on the forest; and if we were ever to leave the smallholding at Laughter and move on to a bigger farm, we needed to build up the herd as fast as possible. So with a great deal of wheedling and helping around the yard, and generally being good, I first got around Mother and then we both worked on Father until he grudgingly allowed Blaze a temporary ticket to Laughter.

The old nagsmen say: 'You have to run through a few bad horses so that you can appreciate getting a good one.' Perhaps it was just beginner's luck, but Blaze was kind from the start and even seemed to seek my company. The memory is still strong after all these years. My Rowan tree with great clusterous berries, flooded in sunlight, and a golden horse standing quietly in between. Blaze and I were soon at work quartering the vast acreage of forest at weekends, holidays and in the evenings when it was light enough to see, herding cattle out of the rack-ways and rides up onto the open ground of Laughter and Bellever tors, the Norway and Sitka spruce nodding and sighing approval in their language inherited from the vast northern wildernesses, perhaps looking kindly on a boy and pony, in contrast to lynx, bear and snow leopard. In the spring when they were clad in virgin green with small brown caps like little finger stalls over the new delicate buds, I would crush the youngest buds between my fingers to smell the fresh pine scent of the bruised tree; and at the fall of the year I would stare up at the high tops with yellow cones hanging like bunches of bananas. Ecologists would class the forestry as a monoculture, but they were benign in a sometimes bleak landscape and they provided areas of valuable shelter for livestock and many species of birds and small mammals that would not have survived on the open heath.

So, as the golden pony and I worked together, so we grew together with a deep trust and understanding based on familiarity and a supposed common purpose. It is modern fashion to use the term 'love' within the human–animal relationship. What is love? It has so many meanings to so many people, but often it seems that the aforesaid ingredients can help create a relationship that is longer lasting and more meaningful than many of the human kind.

FOOD ON THE TABLE

Running beside the work on the holding with its supply of farmyard fare – eggs, milk, butter, cream, vegetables, salted and cured meat – was the need to put fresh meat on the table to supplement the rations and the meagre family income. The most common accessible fresh meat was always rabbit, and the ways of catching bunny were legion. Perhaps the most efficient method was the night light and lurcher, and 'the old man' (Father) was an expert with both. At about that time Father had acquired an 'almost made it' black greyhound called Rose. Rose had gained a reputation for jumping the barrier on the race track, taking a short cut across the middle and waiting at the other side for the hare. Father, no doubt thinking that she showed more brains and sagacity than the average 'long dog', offered her bed and board at Laughter on account that she might help fill the board. Temperament wise, Rose was a yard-and-a-half of grief, but on a good night with the spotlight she was the best in the parish.

I well remember the night Father was sitting in front of the old black kitchen range, cleaning the light (an old headlight taken from a scrapped 16hp Vauxhall) and mounted on a small square board with a leather neck strap and an old light switch – nothing like the new million-candlepower dry-cell lights of today. There was a stiff westerly breeze ten days after the full moon (at that time the moon rises an hour later every night), a whip of rain in the wind and dark as the inside of a cow's guts. Rose had been fasted for the day and knew the old game as well as Father, although at times they both felt that they knew better than the other, and – oh joy – I was allowed to go on condition that I went silently, not seen and definitely not heard. The plan was to cross the East Dart River at Laughter stepping-stones and work the 200 acres of Babeny (farmed at the time by my grandfather).

It had rained heavily earlier in the day, but the river was still low enough to cross. We squelched through the western meadows without much to show for wet feet and on to the higher fields with shorter grass. The light picked up the eyes of the first rabbit fifty yards or so away. Rose, keen for the sport, drummed away following the beam upwind. Bunny, knowing something was amiss but not knowing where the danger was, went 'quat' and flattened himself into the ground 'possum-like', an old trick that had saved many a rabbit over the centuries, while Rose thundered over it. Bunny, realising what was afoot, promptly legged it in the opposite direction back down the light towards us. Rose, having played the game before, spun in a halo of spray and ran back down the light, dazzled but running for sound, chopped it almost at our feet and retrieved to Father's hand who gave it a swift chop behind the ears, which is the only proper way to despatch a rabbit. We hunted the rest of the farm, being careful to work upwind and silently. By the end of the night we had twelve rabbits and two blisters.

The homeward journey was as tiring as twelve rabbits could make it (a good Dartmoor rabbit weighing upwards of three pounds). We thought ourselves well pleased, looking forward to free meat for a day or so – that is, until we came back to the river which over the previous couple of hours had risen considerably. The battery was low, so we had no light but the occasional sliver of moon just rising over Corndon and peeping between the hurrying clouds, showing only the white water where the tips of the stepping-stones broke the heavy glide of the flood. Leaving the now useless light and battery to be collected the next day Father, accompanied by the twelve rabbits, stepped carefully out on to the first stone, water swirling up to his ankles, then the second, and on to the third about mid-stream. Then the moon blinked, there was a heavy splash followed by heavy cursing and the re-illuminated scene of Father half swimming and half plunging towards the far bank with the rabbits bobbing merrily away for Totnes or Dartmouth. Fearing him certainly drowned I sat down hard on a stone and started to blub. Fortunately 'the old man' was not the drowning type. Soon reassurance reached me from the darkness of the opposite bank.

'Stop that noise you silly young bugger and go up to Bellever Bridge, cross and make your way home.' I had assumed he was going to catch the rabbits and come back for me, but evidently one good ducking was enough and the crossing was getting more dangerous by the minute. I was on my own, Father had gone home, rabbits gone south, Rose was swimming and would come out on Father's side perhaps a hundred yards or so downstream (as dogs do when used to fast water), leaving me on the lonely side with a two-mile walk along the banks of the flooded river

Jez's river: the East Dart below Laughter Hole Farm

with only an occasional moonbeam for company. There was nothing for it but to choke back the tears and keep on pegging. Remembering Grandfather's old motto 'Never be afraid of the dark, boy, you will never meet anything uglier than yourself' I plodded on, turning my pockets inside out as a defence against being 'pixie-led', walking as tall as I could and whistling loudly for company until at last I saw the oil-light in the kitchen window. Inside, Father's trousers and coat were steaming on the old black range, Mother was wagging a finger at him, no doubt telling him off for not recrossing the river and drowning the pair of us. But all was not lost as the tight old sod had hung on to a brace of rabbits that Mother would make into a pie in the morning.

After the exercise, excitement and trauma of the rabbiting expedition, followed only by a slice of bread and dripping and a damp bed, the thought of hard-earned rabbit pie the next evening was a treat to look forward to. By the time Father came up the road from Bellever, pushing the bike through the dimpsey, Mother had put the stew pot on with the two rabbits paunched, skinned and cut up into joints with a half pound of salt ham and bacon, minced onion, salt and pepper. This was allowed to simmer for a while in the stock and she then turned the lot into a big pie dish, covered it with pastry, put it back in the oven and within the hour we were all sitting around the old back scullery table, peering at each other through the steam in the flickering light of the oil-lamp and enjoying a good blow out that wouldn't have been bettered by the best hotel in Devon.

Wartime rationing of food and clothing was not long over and meat of any sort was always the best part of any meal, to go with home-grown vegetables. We had rabbit, pigeon, snipe, golden plover, black cock, badger and fish in the autumn. There were no deer on Dartmoor in those days, but badger ham was good meat either fresh or cured. A good adult badger ham would weigh seven or eight pounds and needed careful cooking. The women would soak it well in slightly salty water for five or six hours, wash it off, cover it with pastry and bake it for three or four hours. Eaten with fresh bread, beans and cider sauce it took some beating. Sometimes they would cure badger hams for the winter. Dry salt and sea salt, black pepper, saltpetre and sugar were rubbed in, rubbing and turning every day for about a month, and then drying them and hanging them in muslin in the chimneybreast or any clean, dry place, to be ready in five or six weeks.

Blackcock was rare and I don't remember eating it often, but I think it was roasted like a fowl or capon with good slices of fat bacon over the breast. Pigeon, golden plover and snipe were usually roasted with fat bacon over and a nub of butter inside. The golden plover had the best flavour, but pigeon was more common and easier to shoot. Large flocks would leave the conifers early to raid the lowland clover and stubble fields, coming home to roost late in the evening. They would land in our fields in great numbers for a last snack of clover before going up to bed in the pines. A good double barrel over the hedge would often kill or wound five or six birds.

Badgers (or 'shavers' as they were known, owing to the custom of using their hair for the best shaving brushes) were usually snared in their runs or dug on Sunday mornings. This is not to be confused with badger baiting, which I seem to remember the locals considered to be cruel, unsporting and generally a waste of time and effort. But digging the overpopulated setts where the residents were rooting up the local fields, digging out the hedges, spreading TB and generally causing a nuisance, was a regular Sunday pastime, before church, dinner or pub, depending on individual tastes. At ten o'clock in the forenoon, men armed with picks, mattocks 'twobills' and Devon shovels, with their best terriers and wearing their best boots and leggings, ready to 'go on after', usually hatted and piped, would congregate at the chosen site and let the first dog to ground. The dogs went only one at a time as a second dog, caught up in the excitement, would push his chum into the badger, often resulting in a bad bite or even death. Mr Brock was no slouch, being related to the mink, stoat, white throat and otter, all dangerous adversaries in a tight spot.

The terriers were not supposed to engage the enemy. Their job was to bark and worry the badger, and keep him from digging while the men dug in behind him. The terriers were bred for the sport and enjoyed it so much they seem to live for little else. They mostly had half-cut tails so that when the diggers got close the dog could be drawn back by the tail, while the badger followed until its head came out far enough for a clean shot. A dog that was too brave or foolhardy didn't last long in the game as a badger under close attack will roll up in a ball like a fuzzpig, bringing his teeth up between his back legs to disembowel a dog or snap a hind leg. I can see the faces of the future aghast, hands held up in horror, but for that generation this was part of their life. They neither knew nor wanted any other. Life was basic and hard: they didn't involve themselves in unnecessary cruelty or share the luxury of modern ideas on animal welfare, there wasn't the time or opportunity to study, photograph or agonise over the natural world as society does now. They were part and parcel of the natural world, all looking through the same window, so to speak.

Laughter Hole Farm, 2016

SCHOOLDAYS

'A chill wind of insecurity occasionally crept under the door that had for so long stood between me and a strange and frightening outside world…'

A TIME OF TRANSITION

Those were halcyon days when the ribbon of life stretched endlessly before me, each day an eternity, lightly dusted with sun and security. The war was won and there was a strong class structure running through society. Within that security, as I was growing and feeling my feet, I was starting to notice mild tensions that crept almost unnoticed into the family circle with, on Mother's side, the Cadbury family of chocolate fame

Jez's mother Freda with her dogs, early 1960s. Freda wrote extensively about Dartmoor and was the first advocate for the moor's indigenous hill ponies, battling for recognition of their true value

and, on Father's, tradesmen, smallholders and labourers. The Cadburys were strongly Socialist with a Quaker background and obvious wealth, while the other lot were true blue Tories who were – in today's terms – living well below the poverty line. Needless to say, any early political thoughts I had were confused!

It was probably at about this time of my life that the family tensions came to the forefront and were destined to affect my stable and simple world, and it would not

necessarily be to my advantage. For some time Mother had been working on the assumption that perhaps the life of a farmer-smallholder, the life that I was fast growing into, the life I loved, the life of painted skies, running water, dogs and horses, did not hold the promise of the future that she felt I should aspire to. Bitter arguments were held, Mother maintaining that I should set my sights on at least Dartmouth Royal Naval College or better, and Father recommending a life on the land or forestry. In all the finger wagging and endless arguments I don't ever recall my opinion being solicited. A chill wind of insecurity occasionally crept under the door that had for so long stood between me and a strange and frightening outside world, but eventually Mother's wish that her only child should go out into the world and 'make something of himself' prevailed, as it usually did. After all, her mother, Elsie Pearce, had been locked up with the Pankhursts, fighting for women's suffrage, a London councillor and a Fleet Street journalist. It was a far cry from rabbit pie and three pounds, seventeen shillings and sixpence a week.

The date of execution was set – boarding school! I was to wake at dawn on the first day following the summer holidays and it was all there! The cowardice, the hollow pit in the belly, the welling fear of the unknown. Had I been that lazy, that useless? What had I done wrong? The whortleberries went stale, the birds were silent. Even the dog moped and hung around my feet: what would she do without me? Would she think I had deserted her? Would she in turn think she had done something terribly wrong? Perhaps she would try to follow me across all

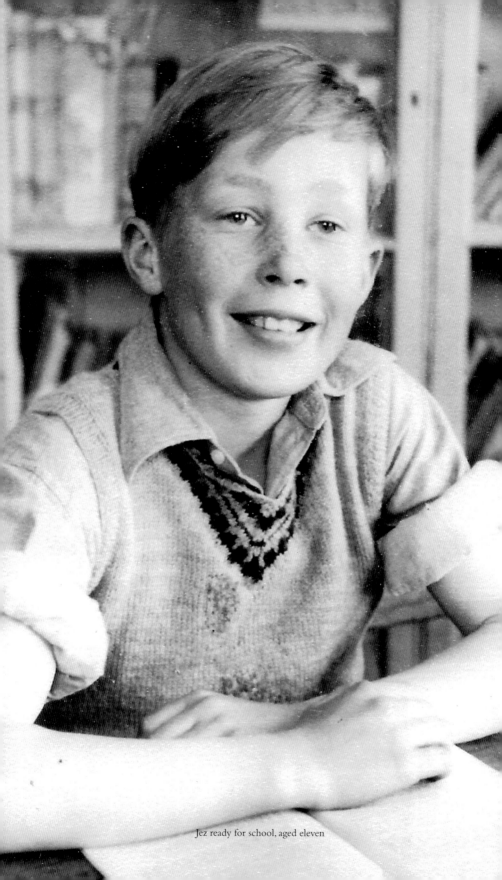

Jez ready for school, aged eleven

those dangerous and lonely miles. I felt that I might as well have been blindfolded, led to a granite wall and shot. On the one hand, I felt I should be brave and British. After all, local boys only fifteen years or so older than me had marched off to fight in the two great conflicts of the century. On the other, I was like the cattle, sheep and ponies, and I didn't want to be driven off my own 'lear' and leave everything that I knew.

The final weeks of summer passed all too quickly. My parents, as if trying to compensate for their betrayal, bought me a new Ingersoll watch and a Raleigh four-speed bicycle with Sturmey Archer gears, and a large red and grey trunk, the latter finally confirming my fear that not only was I being sent away to senior school, but that it was – as I had feared – a far-off boarding school! To fill the grey trunk with the trappings of my future I was taken to a grey town, with grey pavements, grey roofs, grey rain (that came down vertically) and grey tailor's shop, with two sad grey old men shuffling through its intestines and producing grey flannel jackets and grey knickers, which after my initial alarm turned out to be short trousers. Apparently 'the young gentleman would not be allowed to wear long trousers until the third form'.

All at once I was overwhelmed with terrifying and mixed emotions: fear of the unknown, fear of strangers, towns and crowds – and to me, not yet in my teens, a crowd was probably three! Holding grimly to the interesting instruction that I should think myself lucky, I stood trembling on the threshold of a future which held nothing and no one familiar, and a lifestyle that I neither understood nor cared for, or even played lip service to anything that had previously been my world. Enter a lifetime's insecurity!

On the appointed day, I was escorted through the grand granite portals, holding tightly to Mother's hand with the corners of my mouth facing south (those were the first two mistakes), down a long and endless dimly lit corridor with a periphery of sniggering boys. I was delivered to the enemy, who was suitably gowned and mortar-boarded with an expression that should have belonged to an elderly Basset with a touch of gout. The Basset shook hands solemnly and informed me, through half a yard of jowl and spare skin, that I would not be allowed home for at least a month so that I could get over my blubbing and be properly weaned! After the formal unpleasantries my parents left. I was shown my bed and locker (that couldn't be locked in a dormitory of twelve boys), and left to unpack my belongings, seen dimly through a mist of tears. My thoughts hovered between suicide and revenge – fortunately revenge won.

After unpacking, not quite knowing what to do or where to go, I wandered rather nervously through a door marked 'Junior Common Room'. The casual and apparently friendly conversation of a half-dozen or so adolescent boys ceased. One moment of 'fight or flight' indecision and I was overwhelmed by a crushing wave of unfriendly humanity. I was knocked to the floor, relieved of my grey knickers and my underpants, my legs kicked apart and my bits scrubbed with black boot polish. For the next step in my welcome to a house of young gentleman, I was thrown naked under a wall bench and pelted with red hot coals from the Common Room fire, followed by the instruction that if I didn't kick them out to be thrown again I would be beaten by a prefect in front of all —and without the benefit of my trousers. On my first night I slept fitfully, eventually getting to sleep at about 3am.

At about 3.30am I was woken by the wailing of some terrible urban reptile. Two hundred yards from the house was a steep gradient on the main railway line to Cornwall. The through train waited at the bottom of the gradient while its offspring, with an answering wail, chugged out of its siding 'nest' and shoved mother up the hill. Having never heard anything more dangerous than a cow tearing grass outside my bedroom window, I lay for a few minutes terrified until I worked out that it must be mechanical and therefore probably not dangerous.

Breakfast arrived at eight and went again in a cloud of fear and confusion. We were allowed one day's break before school to settle in, so I grabbed my coat and made my way down to old Mother Dart, about a mile away from the boarding house. But she was no longer my river. She had grown wide, fat and slothful. We didn't seem to speak the same language any more; even the oaks that sheltered her banks were fat and portly like old councillors or shamen. I sat in the damp grass under the oldest and wisest of them, taking in the hot sun and the stink of wild garlic while the late swallows skimmed the autumn meadows and a large sleepy fly with a brilliant blue backside sidled slowly around an ivy leaf, enjoying the life-giving warmth. I delayed my return until after dark, but eventually had to rise and make my way back. A wind had got up, not the refreshing breeze of the high moorland but a nasty small-minded town wind with corners, cutting through the sodium halo that cocoons a town and obscures the stars.

The elderly Basset and a senior prefect, obviously believing that I had gone AWOL, were measuring strides in the hallway with severe faces and thumbs in waistcoat sleeves. Perhaps not quite knowing what to do with me, they made the best decision of their day and called Matron. Now Matron Fairweather was a poppet: principled, gentle and everyone's idea of a nice grannie, and although it was late she escorted me into the dining room and produced a small supper, a cup of tea and a slice of kindness that gave me a better night's sleep.

I was up early the next morning, and before any life stirred in the old house I crept out of the dormitory and wandered through the well-manicured lawns. A large ornamental cypress shaded the far corner and provided a residence for two comfortably obese lowland pigeons with a family. I quickly climbed the tree, forgetting the sap and dust spoiling my new grey flannel suit (conifers are filthy trees to climb). Feeling thoroughly at home in the swaying treetop I peered over the flat rough platform of a nest and came face to face with two portly, tufty squabs, not yet fully feathered. Using an old poacher's trick I tethered them to the tree so that they couldn't fly and could be collected later, when fat, for Matron's table. Sadly, Matron was not impressed with the offer of a free meal. She suggested that before she cleaned my suit, I should sneak quietly back and release them.

At 8.15am, after a quick breakfast, we polished shoes, set caps on straight and tightened neckties, proceeding in a long crocodile of thirty or so boys through the town, arriving at school at approximately 8.45am. As with junior school, I could see little point in formal education and I seem to remember I spent most of my time gazing out of the window. I failed to see the relevance of Latin or Greek in the life that I anticipated for myself, 'Amo, Amas, Amat, Amamis, Amatis' and so on. Although a little Latin could be useful for a farmer, I failed to see that at the time.

I idled my way through the first term's lessons, dreaming mostly of home. I collected the record for the swish, was bottom of the class and lost my merit holiday which involved staying on at school while the other boys went home for half term. Thoroughly disgruntled and unhappy, I started sneaking out of the back door and spending my evenings away from the boarding house but somebody snitched on me, resulting in the elderly Basset locking all the doors and windows after dark. But I was one step ahead of that game. Before leaving the boarding house I took a small piece of fine fishing gut, tying it in the handle of the window catch, running it under the frame and outside with a knot in the end. On my return I merely pulled the gut, opening the window catch. I climbed in and carefully returned the gut to my pocket. I was usually in before the Basset's last rounds at 11pm. The grumpy old goat knew there was a tune playing but couldn't quite hear the words.

As to the crimes that normally accompany the cream of England's young gentlemen in a single-sex institution there was, as I remember, little or no homosexual activity, but there was a great deal of bullying. One poor chap in the first year was bullied so badly that eventually in fear of his life he stole a fruit-peeling knife from Matron's table and stabbed an older boy with it. He was a quiet lad, and only slightly different from the rest, but I can still see the fear in his eyes when facing a snarling mob of young gentlemen. The crime, of course, was entirely his own.

There isn't a great deal more to be said about boarding school. I struggled on for a few years remaining at the bottom of the class and retained the record for the swish, until one day I was offered my freedom. 'Old Beefy', the headmaster, summoned me to his study and for the first time treated me like an adult. 'Well, young Wilkinson,' he said, 'you obviously have your mind set on being a bloody peasant. You have learned little or nothing since you have been here with us and we have learned little or nothing from you. Perhaps it would be a good idea if you went home to the farm where you belong!'

I tried very hard to look shamefaced, but the joy in my heart knew no bounds. At the tender age of fourteen, I was being sent back to everything I knew and loved in the real world.

The old blue Hillman van chugged slowly up the drive past the flowering rhododendrons, through the tall ornamental trees, skirting the shaved lawns, and ground to a smoky apologetic halt in the deep gravel outside the front door. It smelled wonderfully of sheep, wet sacking and Stockholm tar, and the dear old dog with her snotty nose jammed against the window. The groundsman, with an authoritative wave, sent it around to the tradesman's entrance where it would obviously feel more comfortable. Only Father had come for me and the journey home was completed in a strained silence, but little I cared, although apparently Mother was left at home in tears over my failure to become a young gentleman. Our route home to the high moor precisely reversed the route of the old river from its source.

Just before my triumphant return, having beaten the system (as I saw it then), my grandfather had retired and bought a small farm in the village of Poundsgate behind the pub (which suited him up to the ears) and my parents had moved into the farm that he vacated, known as Babeny. Babeny is part of the estate of the Duchy of Cornwall and one of Dartmoor's few remaining 'ancient tenements'. I had known Babeny well as a child and was familiar with all its nooks and crannies so, as a move, it was not as dramatic as leaving Dartmoor would have been. I was sad to wave goodbye to Laughter but it meant a tenfold increase in acreage and as the move had been anticipated for quite some time, my familiarity with the house and farm obviously eased the transition.

As the old van chugged wearily up all the hills from Ashburton, my sense of coming home to my own lear mounted until we reached the summit of Sherril Hill, where I asked Father to stop so that I could get out and enjoy the best view in England. Beside me a skylark sprang from the heather. It ascended up and up until it was just a tiny dot in the sky, singing its tiny heart out and then dropping back step by step to the warm earth. I think that perhaps I had never heard anything quite so beautiful (although many decades later I had the privilege of listening to Dame Kiri Te Kanawa singing in St Paul's Cathedral at the wedding of Prince Charles and that came a close second). I stood at the top of the hill for long minutes and beat my arms across my chest in the chill breeze, while gazing across the old valley to Babeny and Laughter. Nothing was said, but I believe we were both concerned about how to console Mother and secure the long-term future of the farm.

The view towards Yar Tor from the hillside above Babeny

BABENY

'The very next morning I started work.
I had assumed I would return like the
prodigal son, but there was no fatted calf.
I was given the same working hours as
a farm labourer…'

WORK THE HEALER

The very next morning I started work, with the accompanying comment from Father that I might have been a lazy bugger at school, but here he would see to it that I had no choice. I had assumed I would return like the prodigal son, but there was no fatted calf. I was given the same working hours as a farm labourer, remuneration ten shillings (50p) a week and my keep, and if I did not like it I could keep walking. No problem, I thought. Let me at it!

I found that the tempo of farming had changed and there was a greater urgency. The old Fordson Major tractor had been replaced by a small Ferguson T20, a tidy little tractor in smart grey livery, part of the Ferguson agricultural system. It ran on a mixture of petrol and tractor vaporising oil (TVO) and it had a neat little hole in the front for a starting handle (not much use on the 200hp tractors of today). It was also open to the elements, and learning to be a tractor driver in the cold rain and sleet of a Dartmoor spring took a little of the romance out of the situation.

Jez driving his first tractor – a Fergie T20, 'open to the elements' – 1960

But learn I had to. 'Fergie' had a small, light two-furrow plough and learning to adjust the depth, set and pitch was an art in itself and deeply satisfying when you got it right. The smell of the freshly turned earth and the shine on the furrow left by the mouldboard, and solving puzzles generated by small awkwardly shaped fields liberally sprinkled with granite boulders, was a joy. (In those days the ploughshares were made of cast iron and frequently broke when they came up hard against a rock.) Living in a valley it was important to get your furrow straight as all the neighbours could see and there was no better joke on a market day than crooked ploughing: the bar of the market house inn would reverberate with clever neighbours 'taking the mick'.

FIRST LOVE

At about this time while in my mid teens and feeling a lack of company of my own age, I decided to go to the local youth club down in the village. There wasn't much youth in those days, probably between twelve and fifteen youngsters from the two local villages. At the club I enjoyed my first social interaction with girls and blew my mind with the amazing discovery that girls had three interesting physical areas that were different from us boys. My curiosity was particularly taken by a very pretty small blonde of about fourteen or fifteen summers. She was semi-local, all her bits were in the right place and beautifully developed, and she seemed to have a passing interest in me. It was love at first sight for me! From that moment, I determined to get a 'fern ticket' to transport us through the long summer evenings. Now there is only one place to get a genuine fern ticket in early summer and that is from the local pixies. This ticket will allow the bearer, or bearers, to creep quietly away from the rest of humanity and make a comfortable couch among the tall ferns. In many areas, the ferns are as thick as the bristles on a pig's back and stand up to six feet high. It was on one of these pixie couches on an evening in higher summer when, together, we experienced a shattering and almost frightening pelvic explosion that would change our lives forever.

As we were both of an agricultural persuasion the operation had proceeded swiftly and efficiently to its conclusion. Shortly after this the enormity of the act hit me and I was left with the interesting problem of controlling my palpitating heart and shaking fingers while I endeavoured to repackage the beautiful slim young body, ivory skinned, served but once and beautiful in its naïveté, into various layers including a liberty bodice, green serge knickers and heavy woollen socks. It is amazing how incriminating bits of dried bracken and dead grass insinuate themselves into heavy woollen socks!

From that moment on, we were firm friends and spent summer evenings with buttercups under chins, holding hands, playing silly games and doing all the things that young country lovers do. It was one evening in our first winter that youth club night found Sherrill valley snowed in. The road was icy and there was a vicious east wind. In those days we only had two-wheel drive vehicles but I was so 'loved up' that, against Father's advice, I'd decided walk the three miles to the village hall.

When the table tennis, chatter and general teenage business was finished, I set out to walk home. It was the last quarter of the moon, which gave a pale half light. One third of the way home at the top of Bell Tor Hill I had a strange experience, the memory of which will stay with me for the rest of my life. I was passing the road that comes up from Rowbrook when I saw, coming out of the side road, a tall man in a black coat with an old cloth cap, striding purposefully towards me out of the snow. I knew the residents of Rowbrook valley well, as friends and neighbours, and I knew all the local farmers and cottagers for miles around. The man was only visible to me for about three or four yards; he was a complete stranger and walked straight at me. It was snowing heavily and I greeted him loudly with a shout, partly from fear and partly thinking that perhaps he was lost. He didn't attempt to turn aside and should have collided heavily with my shoulder, but with fixed features and staring, almost frightened eyes he walked straight through me. Badly frightened, I turned and shouted after him! He walked on into eternity, a strange tall black figure disappearing into the blizzard, but not a snowflake on him, nor footprint behind him.

I questioned locals, neighbours and most of the older residents for a while afterwards but nobody had heard of a stranger at Rowbrook or even in the parish on that night.

Strangers were a great novelty in those days, perhaps one or two a year, and would have been well recorded at church, pub or whist drive. It is only now, more than fifty years later, that I learn from Patrick Simpson, the current Lord of the Manor, that there used to be a gibbet on that spot many years ago!

WINTER 1962/63

It was Boxing Day. The turkey had been demolished, the Christmas pudding had been eaten and the Christmas cake had been sampled (to placate Grandma). The dogs were lying around the fire like stinking fish, too full of leftovers to squabble. The words 'benign' and 'replete' would adequately describe the company, both human and canine. It was early evening, getting on for dark, when I decided rather unkindly to dig the dogs out of their stupor. We took the ancient driftway, leaving Babeny for the higher moor of Riddon Ridge. Traditionally we would have spent Boxing Day rabbiting with ferret and nets, but we had skipped rabbiting and the dogs were in need of exercise. It would make a good story to say that the dogs were nervous and preoccupied and that I had some inclination of what was to follow, but it was a quiet evening and we arrived home tired and happy, and went early to bed.

Deep snow in the farmyard drifted up to the roofs and blocked doorways at Babeny.
Jez can just be seen on the drift (centre) digging his way in to the calves

The next morning I woke late. The bedroom ceiling was a lighter shade of pale. I shot to the window and looked out. It was snowing heavily with a strong breeze and it was difficult to see across the yard, but as Babeny lies in a hollow, the yard looked pretty well drifted in. One particular drift reached nearly to the sill of the bedroom window, curling over at the top like a breaker in an ocean of snow! Unlike an ocean, the snow was deathly silent.

It snowed for the whole of the next day and into the night. By the second morning, the wind had dropped and eventually through that day the snow finally stopped. By this time we had struggled out across the yard, up to our waists in snow, to feed the cows and young cattle in the nearer sheds. Our own supplies were adequate. In those days we had plenty of salt pork and ham, salt beans, swedes and potatoes in clamps and so on. The main worry was the outlying stock. We had 250 Scotch half-bred sheep out on the higher moor. They would have been sheltering between Babeny and Bellever, probably under Snails House covert, anything up to two miles upriver. The gates were drifted in, only the tops being visible, and there was no way to reach the sheep apart from walking. Just to complicate matters, the wind changed to a cold northeasterly and a very hard frost had set in.

As there was no way of getting food to the sheep, the only option was to find the sheep and bring them home to the yard. While Mother stayed, quite literally to keep the home fires burning, Father and I with two dogs (after equipping ourselves with two long sticks) left the yard at around mid morning to see how many of the sheep we could find. Walking up the driftway to the moor gate was comparatively easy going, apart from clambering over the drifts. We walked over the gate and set out heading north across the top of the ridge, but once we got out onto the open moor we found that the frozen snow crust overlying the heather and gorse would only support our weight for one step in three, and the other two were spent floundering up to our waists in snow and filling our boots: result, wet feet and wet backsides.

The dogs thought it was a great game and gambolled in the snow playing bulldozers. Eventually we struggled as far as Snails House wall. The snow had drifted very deep here under the shelter of the pines. We started to probe with our long sticks into the drifts, occasionally finding a soft spot where the sheep had huddled together in the shelter and the snow had drifted over them. The heat of their bodies had formed perfect little igloos with thick ice walls.

Eventually, after several days, Father had lost a great deal of weight and looked grey with fatigue and worry. A significant part of a lifetime's work and a large slice of the future lay under the frozen snow. We struggled on for the best part of a week, our only company the black scavenging crows and the nasty tempered malignant blackthorns, hard-prickled and sullen, protruding from the icy crust with their backs to the weather that had crippled them from youth. Even Dartmoor's small wild people – the rabbits, mice, moles – were frozen underground and it was many weeks before we saw the tell-tale stains of brown earth around small holes in the drifts, indicating life under the ice.

In the late evenings we were treated to a rare show of the Northern Lights, strange and wonderful sheets and waves of coloured light hovering and flickering in the early night sky. For each bunch of sheep that we dug out, we trampled a circle of snow and left them there to be picked up later. As time went on we started to find bunches of sheep that had been eating each other's fleeces in their icy prisons; the poor things were starving and some of them were almost bald.

By the end of the week we had most of the sheep on the surface. The next problem was to get them home. By now they were getting weak, and every time they tried to struggle out of the deep snow, they would break through the frozen crust and their fleeces would hold them down until they became exhausted and gave up. With two bleak miles to go the situation looked impossible, but eventually we hit on a plan. Old Mother Dart had come to our rescue! She was frozen to a depth of nine inches to a foot, with another foot or so of smooth snow lying on top of the ice. The Dartmoor

The East Dart river froze to a foot thick in the winter of 1962/63

ponies were managing to walk through the snow on the moor and were busily digging for the heather and dead grass. So the next morning, I brought old Blaze out on to the moor. He supervised while we dug a path down to the river, which at that point was not too far. With Father breaking a trail down the centre of the river and all the sheep following as sheep do, Blaze, the dogs and I brought up the rear. It was strange to walk on top of the old river ('walking on water' not being quite my forte), and where the scrambling sheep had scuffed the snow Blaze was alarmed and intrigued at the sight of the bubbles of air travelling under the ice: a new experience for both of us.

There had been a freezing mist in the valley overnight and all the tiny gorse prickles and twiglets on the trees were covered in a thin layer of ice, locally known as ammil, so when the northerly breeze combined with the occasional rays of sunshine, the whole valley lit up with all the sparkling colours of the rainbow and tinkled like a thousand tiny chimes.

In those days the telephone wires were carried above ground between poles, and nearer civilisation, where there were many wires, the ammil coated them as thick as your finger and produced enough weight to snap some off the telephone poles. In the frozen silence they sounded like rifle shots. Anyway, 'the moving finger writes', and we eventually arrived home with most of the sheep but there was a decided absence of 'piety nor wit' (from Omar Khayyam [AD1048–1131]: Persian mathematician, astronomer, philosopher and poet).

It is difficult to explain to the modern urban mind the nagging ever-present fear of failure, starving stock and bankruptcy, with no easy option of living comfortably by begging from society, claiming benefits under some flimsy pretext. There were no excuses in the middle of the last century, and perhaps we could do with a few less at the start of this one.

We carried on searching for sheep through most of January. I regularly carried the old .22 rifle on a strap over my shoulder, basically for humane euthanasia, and I remember one evening, trudging back from the top of Riddon Ridge, when I was quite glad of its reassurance. The wind had dropped, all the moor was a desert of white silence and as I passed the top of Snails House plantation I counted fourteen foxes line astern. They had crossed the frozen river from Bellever and struggled up through Snails House and out on to the deep snow of the ridge, intent on doing the same job as us (digging out dead sheep). The hair stood up on the back of my neck. They were presumably two or three litters of last year's cubs, helping each other out in extreme conditions, but to me they looked for all the world like a pack of hunting wolves.

I swung around dropping to one knee and took careful aim, killing the first fox

Feeding sheep at Babeny early in 1963, after digging them out and bringing them home

in its tracks. The rest scattered. Presumably they were as surprised to see me as I was to see them.

That picture will remain with me. One scene in a timeless play acted out over so many centuries. Starving carnivores and helpless prey animals, both fighting for existence in thousands of acres of endless snow, with tiny stars pricking the night sky and me, an impartial observer at that frozen moment, holding the power of life and death over both. All of us tiny specks of life, alive for that fraction of time in a world as inhospitable, remote, silent and alien as the fastnesses of time and space itself.

But all bad things must eventually come to an end and the '63 winter was no exception. After a little over three months the sun rose a little higher in the sky each day and at long last we saw a tiny plume of smoke over the top of Sherrill Hill. We watched it for half a day and eventually under the smoke appeared the roof of a large yellow Caterpillar tractor. I am sure Mother had never seen a more welcome sight in her life, and even Father looked relieved.

The thaw had set in and in the wind-blown patches the occasional blade of new green grass was bravely pushing upward through the melting snow. But of course the thaw brought its own problems. Sherrill Hill was a complete flood, running from top to bottom in its own channel many feet deep, rivulets from the melting drifts adding to the torrent on the way down. The little hay that we had left in the tallets was sodden below the melting snow that had blown up under the slates; there was as much snow in the tallets as there was on top of the roofs. As almost all the fodder on Dartmoor was exhausted and much of the farm was a sea of mud, the government used the army helicopters to fly in fodder. This was dropped from the air, but most of it was thistles and docks. It probably made an interesting spicy curry for the animals, but it was not very nutritious.

Gradually, the familiar landmarks, gates and fences started to reappear. After so long under a white shroud the landscape appeared unfamiliar and strange. Earlier each morning the birds started to sing again and the sheep that we had saved from the snow began to lamb. The great surge of spring was upon us; the millions of tiny unborn buds and shoots were stirring under the warming earth. Redcurrant and elder came first, then the foetal shoots on the end of the hazel wands appeared like tiny green moths beside the virgin green of the young beech. Our whole world was slowly being reborn.

It was a west wind, the warm wind, which coaxed Dartmoor out of that winter. Great patches of shade and sunlight chased each other, driven by the wind across the face of the moor, punctuated by the wild cries of curlew and plover sweeping into the marshes. All of a sudden the hibernation was over; all the small people were busy again about their domestic affairs, the pied wagtails (or 'dishwashers' as we called them) rushing about with beakfuls of insects to stuff into the tiny scarlet trumpets that were arranged too close for comfort in a deep nest under the bridge. Plump young rabbits amused themselves in the early sunshine by playing chicken between hedge and bramble patch and telling each other outrageous stories about how they had survived the winter, watched carefully by the buzzards and crows that were all replete on carrion and couldn't decide whether fat young bunnies were really worth the effort. Gradually life returned to normal and we got used to going out of the valley again.

The Thaw

Hungry vixen, ears a-twitch,
You stalk the bramble covered ditch,
Where silver ripple runs no more,
While snipe grow bold the cattle roar,
And our oldest enemy snuffs at the door.

Jez Wilkinson

TO THE LOWLANDS

As the year progressed it was difficult sometimes to remember how hard the winter had been, although while travelling about the moor we were constantly reminded by the piles of bones and skulls that were to be found under the lee side of some of the hedges and reaves. We had been very lucky; we had only lost a few sheep. All the cattle and ponies were safe but unfortunately, along with the damp hay in the tallet, the few remaining swede and teddy pits were stinking, rotten and useless.

Clarence's South Devons, 1950s (before de-horning became usual practice)

The lack of suitable fodder necessitated an early migration to the south for all the cattle. We were lucky enough to have some rented land near Torbay in the village of Daccombe. This was nearly at sea level and consequently grew grass much earlier than we did on Dartmoor.

In the old days livestock from the lowlands was driven up to Dartmoor for the summer using the old driftways from the lowland parishes of the South Hams, a spring migration principally from the Kingsbridge and Totnes areas. This enabled the farmers of the lower land to save more winter fodder. But in our case it was either find early grass or starve, so we did it back to front as it were.

I remember just as the herd was leaving the farm gate at Babeny we noticed one cow had two extra feet sticking out of the business end. She had to stay behind and she got herself in a terrible state shut in the yard while all her friends were going on holiday to Torbay. Unfortunately with the stress and commotion she took a long time to settle

71

down to calving and she had a hard time of it. The calf was presented correctly, but it was very large in the hips, and Father and I had to pull it off with ropes. Consequently the poor old cow suffered trauma in the nerves and muscles of one hind leg and couldn't stand. After delivering the rest of the herd we returned home to deal with the invalid. I remember we spent days 'merging into weeks' feeding and watering her, and keeping her warm with a rug. We used the tractor and loader to stand her up on her feet every day and in between she lay looking at us with an expression that betrayed neither fear, anger or even recognition. Father swung through a range of emotions, from the desire to help and protect the injured and helpless in his charge, to anger at a stupid animal that wouldn't or couldn't try to help herself. I think perhaps it was the first time that I had seen Father cry tears of frustration.

The calf had suffered tremendous pressure during parturition and was bleeding from the back end. The old man's experience told him that the calf would die and that we would have to shoot the cow, but he didn't let on to either Mother or me. A young cow and big bull calf represented a large slice of the year's income, and their combined ages could mean a wait of six or seven years to breed replacements. So any small shop-bought luxuries or holidays would have to wait. Agricultural supplies and the rent came first.

The early grass at Daccombe was a double-edged sword, On the one side the cows relished the fresh grass that waved ankle deep on the hill above Barton Road. For a time it was a much better life than picking penny pies out of the granite walls at Babeny. (We called the small green leaves of pennywort peeping through crevices in the walls 'penny pies'. They were circular and where the stalk met the leaf it sometimes looked as if a slice had been removed. In fact Peter called any animal that had a pointed or snipe nose that would probe between the granite rocks a 'penny pie picker'.) Be that as it may, the second edge of the sword was a new range of bovine problems ranging from summer mastitis to ragwort poisoning, and of course every new ailment necessitated a round trip of forty miles. But at least the cows were well fed and happy.

Ragwort is, according to the government, a 'noxious weed', and I think it is illegal to grow it or to allow it to grow on your property. Now, forty or so years later, the government and local councils allow it to grow in gay profusion everywhere. It is of course highly poisonous, more so when cut and slightly dried or wilted. Many thousands of cattle and horses have died from ragwort poisoning over the years. It attacks the liver and sometimes does not manifest itself for months, or even years. I have on occasion bought horses showing every appearance of health and vigour only to have them die on me a good while later. Grazing animals always seem to be much healthier and thriftier when they are periodically moved to different soils. I guess apart from the change of scenery they also pick up different minerals and the like. But I suppose even grumpy old farmers probably benefit from a small holiday by the sea, and overlooking the sea was our only recompense for the several days that we had to spend picking ragwort through the summer months. It is very hard to pull in dry soil and every little piece of root that breaks off below the surface will grow into a new plant next year.

We were lucky enough to employ a man to take care of the cows when they were calving which left us at home to look after the sheep while they took centre stage for lambing. The lambing was difficult that year, possibly because the sheep had been upset and had to struggle through the deep snow. Many of the lambs were arriving breech, upside down or with one leg back, and if the ewe was having twins the complications could be manifold and needed a great deal of time and patience to unravel. The foxes were still hungry after the hard winter and their predations accounted for twenty or twenty-five percent of the lamb flock that year. In those days we had no sheds to keep the ewes in, and in desperation we resorted to all sorts of tricks to try and keep the foxes away. As the lambs were born we marked them with strong-smelling Stockholm tar and we urinated on them – in fact we tried anything that we thought would give them a strange smell that would put the foxes off, but mostly to no avail. We even stayed up all night in the lambing field, sitting in the old van with the dogs for company and old storm lanterns hanging around the edges of the field, but the foxes were crafty.

One of their favourite tricks was to single out a ewe with a young double. One fox would draw the ewe away with the stronger lamb while its partner sneaked in behind the ewe and killed its smaller sibling. Sometimes an older badger would join in the feast. You could always tell a lamb that a badger had killed. It would be left spread-eagled upside down, usually with just the soft stomach and its milky contents torn out.

CHASING FOXES – AND THE WHITE WITCH

Our hatred for foxes in those days knew no bounds. We killed them in every way that we could. Snaring, shooting, poisoning and hunting were all legitimate ways of protecting the flock. Naturally enough it was not long before I decided that I would like to go hunting in earnest. I had been hunting in a basket saddle with Mother on the end of a rope since the tender age of three (somewhere I still have a photograph to prove it). Even in those days I had a glass in my hand. Hunting in the sixties was

Jez hunting with the Dart Vale at Dunnabridge, aged four: 'Even in those days I had a glass in my hand!'

enjoyed by many tenant farmers and farm labourers – not exactly an elite sport! Whenever the hunt passed through, it was an excuse to down tools and take a few minutes' break to watch.

With Mother's help I kitted myself out with all the correct clothing. Blaze was also sorted out like the hunter he thought he should be. When his feet were polished, his mane and tail plaited and his coat groomed until it shone, he thought himself a very fine gentleman.

There was of course in the farming and labouring community no sympathy for the foxes. They were threatening our livelihood and we chased them as you would chase a man that had stolen your wallet, and believe me the rangy hill fox took some chasing. Every few hundred yards Dartmoor supplied a clitter of rocks or a badger's sett as a refuge. Some of our best runs were in the spring of the year, 'klickiting time', when the dog foxes could be found many miles from home with a bunch of flowers and their pants around their ankles so to speak. When disturbed they would hightail it for more familiar ground back on their own lear. 'The uneatable pursued by the unspeakable' they might have been, but they often provided a long run over hard country testing the courage of both riders and horses. Some of the hardest riders and most courageous were the kids. It was not unusual to see experienced middle-aged gentleman riding hard over rough country, on big raw-boned Thoroughbred-type hunters, suffering the indignity of being overtaken by a small female child on a scruffy Dartmoor pony with her legs stuck out horizontally and her pigtails flying in the breeze. (Strangely enough scruffy Dartmoor ponies often crossed their native territory with a great deal more aplomb than expensive heavyweight hunters.)

There was one particular incident that I remember well. We met at Bellever Bridge and the Dartmoor were hunting on an unpleasant November day with a sting of sleet in the easterly wind. We soon found a travelling fox in the deep covert beside the village. He was presumably a dog fox from the high plateau because he took a straight line over Bellever Tor, crossing the main Princetown to Moretonhampstead road, running through the bogs at Powdermills. He then swung out right-handed heading for Fernworthy plantation. After struggling up the heavy going towards Archerton, Blaze was blowing hard, but the scent was good. Hounds were screaming away into the middle distance, the Master and one or two of the thrusting field had gone with them, and in order to follow Blaze and I had to negotiate a three-foot granite wall on to Archerton newtake. His blood was up and he charged the wall like an old timer. Unfortunately the ground was churned up by the previous riders, and on take-off Blaze's hind legs sank. We landed in an undignified and muddy heap, with himself lying on my leg and thrashing at the remnants of the granite wall with his hind legs. When we eventually struggled to our feet, the rest of the field had galloped on to Fernworthy leaving us rather alone. On inspection and to my horror I found hot blood spurting from Blaze's stifle. I wiped away the peaty slime to discover a nasty cut on the inside of his hind leg, big enough to hide two fingers.

Standing there in the cold sleet with no company and my boy likely to bleed to death was not my idea of a good day. I ripped off my stock, wrapping it tightly around the cut. The bleeding continued unabated. My tie, saturated with blood, slipped down to his hock taking my courage and spirits with it. My mind was in a whirl, but occasionally, in extremis, the brain seems to run on overdrive and I remembered that just down the road there lived a white witch. It was well known in the locality that she could cure warts, ringworm and the like. She was also known as a 'blood healer'. So both of us, limping badly in sibling sympathy, made our sorry way down to the smallholding.

We were immediately 'jointly and severally' attacked by a flock of angry geese and a pack of scabby dogs, closely followed by a very elderly woman, bent double

View across Postbridge and up the East Dart valley: Archerton land to the left, middle distance

with age and tribulation. The old girl stared hard at us with rheumy eyes that whispered cataract, but were sharp enough to immediately take in the situation. I was a little nervous in case it was her wall that we had demolished and she would send us away with a flea in our ear, but we were in luck. Mumbling something about 'that bloody young oik from Laughter', she bent down and examined the pony. While stroking his flank with one claw she closed the lips of the cut with the other. The bleeding eased temporarily, but as soon as Blaze moved, the regular pulse of an arterial bleed broke through again, spurting on to the black peat. Seeing this, the old girl took the headpiece from me, hissing something about staying where I was and not 'getting in the damned way'. She led Blaze into a dirty old shed that looked like a cross between a cart linhay and a calves' house. Fearing for Blaze's safety (and not being very good at doing as I was told) I sidled up to the grubby window and peered through, just in time to see the old girl take a large handful of cobwebs from the ceiling and hold them firmly against the cut. It must have been a full half an hour later that she remerged with Blaze, amazingly sound and no longer bleeding. I could not have been more relieved and thanked her profusely. I guess magic, like the good Lord, helps them that help themselves, and I held my peace about the cobwebs for many a year.

CHARACTERS IN THE FIELD

I am not now – nor ever have been – inclined towards the admiration of other men, but back in those testosterone-filled teenage years, the man that was hunting hounds that day, one Dennis Ferrens, stood head and shoulders above any of the other horsemen of my acquaintance. Dennis was a man of private means and farmed near Ipplepen. He was master and huntsman of both the Dartmoor and South Devon hounds at various times. He had been a leading amateur rider in his day along with Mildmay-White of Flete. As I scampered along on Blaze in the wake of the great man on his 17-hand hunter he seemed to be all the things that I aspired to. His deeds were legendary, his style, courtesy and manners were impeccable, and a good percentage of the hunting ladies loved him to distraction.

There was one particular occasion that I remember when I was not hunting. I was a passenger in someone else's Land Rover and we were stuck in traffic, buried in a deep narrow country lane. The fields above and below were steeply sloping, and hounds had found their fox in deep cover above Halsanger. Running mute and straining every sinew, down they came from the steep fields above, dropping some six feet into the lane and crossing just in front of us. There was not a gate in sight! Dennis cantered purposefully down the field. With Ambrose, his favourite hunter, judging his stride perfectly and taking off close above us, they sailed serenely over both lane and Land Rover landing safely in the field below. And just for a touch of style the old blighter doubled his horn as he went over. No wonder they loved him!

Ambrose of course was the favourite only for that generation. Before him there had been Rose o' May, a cracking little mare who had distinguished herself both in the hunting and steeplechasing field. I can recall one remarkable incident when I was still very small. Dennis was riding Rose o' May at the Dunnabridge point-to-point races, and in those days the fences were made by laying birch over the granite walls – not a practice that would be recommended by the health and safety authorities of today.

Well on into the race the mare fell, catapulting Dennis into the wall, depriving him of consciousness and a couple of front teeth. The mare galloped on for maybe ten to twenty lengths then, realising that her 'lord and master' was no longer with her, she abandoned the race and trotted back to stand over him. I don't think I have seen such a show of affection from a horse in extreme conditions either before or since. But of course his horses, like his women, loved him to distraction. They were beaten regularly when they became opinionated (the horses, not the women!) and rewarded well for their noble efforts.

The equestrian world occasionally throws up a few people with that extra sense of perception that allows them to share the mind of a young horse. The modern generation has invented the term 'horse whisperer', but many of the older horsemen like Dennis, who were brought up with horses, either were born with or developed this gift. A young horse will usually look for friendship and leadership, as will a young human, and the wise horseman, with kindness, firmness and patience, can often fill this role.

Another great character of the hunting field in those far-off times was Gillian Howard. Gillian used to act as amateur whip to Dennis. She was the daughter of Sir John Shelley, who had large estates in the Crediton area. A day's hunting was always great fun when Gillian was out. Although no longer in the first flush of youth she was a brave horsewoman with a dry sense of humour and would have been described by us youngsters as an 'old hard-arse'.

I particularly remember one day when Gillian's sharp sense of humour came to the fore and amused us all, apart from the poor recipient. Gillian had been riding a particularly flighty young five-year-old on a wet day. The youngster had been playing up all day and had given Gillian a hard time. Unfortunately we had that day been particularly blessed with the presence of three young yuppies from Sloane Square. Gillian had already been heard at the meet mumbling into her glass something about 'puppies' being a better description and at the end of the day both madam and horse were sweating profusely, and neither in the best of tempers. Just before we boxed the horses one young buck, thinking himself to be a gentleman, wandered over to Gillian and exclaimed: 'By God, ma'am, your horse is sweating well. I'd say you gave it a damned fine ride for a lady of your age.'

Gillian fixed him with a steely blue grey gaze emanating from a face reminiscent of a walnut with attitude. 'Young man,' said she, 'had you spent the last six hours between my legs you would be bloody sweating as well! And I doubt that you would be as fine a ride!' Game set and match.

In the days when most agricultural work was done manually and the winter days were long and tedious, the standard winter clothing (if one aspired to anything more modern than a hessian sack) was usually not waterproof. The hours of wet and cold seemed to drag on interminably, so when the wild cry of hounds echoed down the valley both farm animals (as in horses and dogs) and farm workers all took a welcome break, happy to watch thirty or forty fit horses careering down a rough Dartmoor valley in pursuit of Charles Fox. It was possibly the best and only entertainment of the winter, especially as many of the farm children and agricultural workers could ride with greater tenacity and knowledge of the country than most of the visitors. The icing on the cake was the sight of a visitor falling off in the gorse or mud.

The daughter of a famous publisher comes to mind: tears, temper tantrum and so on. Consequently hunting was tremendously popular in all the areas on and around Dartmoor. I don't believe it was particularly a class thing, as many of the local tenant farmers, their families and the farm workers regularly joined in with the hunt. After all, foxes being carnivores following their natural pattern of life inevitably decimated the local hen runs and lambing fields, and if your livelihood depends on culling your enemy, you may just as well have fun doing it.

Hunting was of course often responsible for emptying the wallets of many a successful man and ruining the reputation as of many a 'faithful and trustworthy' wife!

THE FIRST TIME

It was at about this time of my life – at the grand old age of nineteen – I fell deeply in love, and against the advice of my parents and family decided that it would be a good idea to get married, my bride being the sixteen-year-old only daughter of a family of local pixie makers. We had been 'stepping out' for some considerable time and although we were both very young I suppose we were trying to rebel and, in our naïveté, I believe we both felt that our individual home backgrounds left a lot to be desired. When you are in your teens it is amazing how stupid and short-sighted your parents are. But the words of old Peter Hannaford always haunt me. 'When you are in your mid-teens your father is a bloody fool. By the time you get to twenty he seems to have learned a little, and by the time you are twenty-five it is just amazing how much the old bugger has learned.'

When we were first married we moved into a small flat in Ashburton and there were younger families living both above and below us. After Babeny I found the atmosphere claustrophobic, money was very tight and I longed for the open spaces of Dartmoor. I took a job with a local forestry company at a weekly wage of £28 and, with groceries at £8 per week and rent at £15, there was not much left. As Mr Micawber might have the said, 'Result: stress'. To supplement our wage I sold firewood from door to door around Ashburton and Buckfastleigh, and the forestry company kindly let me keep some pigs in their heavy beech woods around the fringes of Dartmoor. Pigs being one farming enterprise that multiplies very quickly (possibly twenty young a year from each sow) I soon managed to get up to over

Old and 'new' bridges at Dartmeet, just above the confluence of East and West Dart rivers

one hundred pigs. I fed them mostly on swill, which I collected from hotels around Torbay and Newton Abbot. It was a messy business and I was not very welcome at close quarters in the local pub, but the pigs liked it and grew fat. It was amazing to see a herd of pigs fighting and squealing over a long trough full of swill. It was complete bedlam, and yet at the end of their feed time they would leave tiny slivers of glass and razor blades and all sorts of sharp objects licked clean at the bottom of the trough. As far as I know, no pig ever swallowed a foreign body, or yet left me a diamond ring.

But the sidelines kept the wolf from the door, so to speak, and eventually we managed to rent an old Dartmoor longhouse, a bleak granite house called Oldsbrim, set high on the moor between Poundsgate and Dartmeet. It was thatched, but the thatch had deep black holes in it edged with the green slime that can be seen adorning the lips of peat bog holes in the west of Ireland. The walls were four feet thick, built of granite and filled with damp rubble, and there was an interesting groove chiselled into the granite floor running the length of the house to take the water that ran down the walls out of the front door.

But in those days we had to take whatever accommodation we could get and we were young and healthy, and as is usual with most young couples the future always looks bright. By this time we had been blessed with an addition to our family. Young Paul was a delicate spark to kindle a new generation.

It was at this stage of my life that the implacable journeyman Fate dealt us a hand of sadness. For my wife it was possibly the greatest sadness that a young woman would ever have to endure. The first card was a violent early autumn storm. The high winds and rain came thrashing through the woods, bringing down the green acorns and beech mast from the oak and beech trees. All the sow pigs were heavy with young at that time and they gorged themselves on the acorns. Unfortunately the chemical composition of the green acorns made them abort – and just as we were expecting our first crop of piglets, we were faced with literally hundreds of small dead or half-alive foetuses scattered around the woods. The loss of that winter's crop of course pleased the foxes and badgers, but made things very tight for us financially, and as there were no social benefits in those days we had to cut back drastically on heating and home comforts. The old house only had one open fireplace which we fuelled with logs through the evening, but this went out in the night and left the house cold and damp.

The next card dealt must have been the ace of hell. I remember rising early one morning, and letting the dogs out into the cold and dark, looking back at the old house from the yard. The old place seemed to be squatting malevolently against the backdrop of the moorland skyline, glaring at me under heavy thatched eyebrows. After feeding the dogs, I went back into the house and made a cup of tea for both of us. I tiptoed upstairs with the tea and laid it quietly on the bedside table beside my young wife as she lay curled on her side, sleeping peacefully like a kitten. Next I went in to the little room that we had decorated as a nursery for Paul.

He was lying on his back, strangely quiet, with a touch of blue around his lips and sightless eyes staring uncomprehendingly at the ceiling. As a farmer I was used to death, but I stood for a long time trying to understand why our lives had been torn apart and trying to pluck up the courage to take on the job that I knew I must do. There can't be many harder jobs for a married man than having to tell his young wife that her baby lies only a few feet away with the small flame of life extinguished for eternity.

Paul had lost the great battle for life that symbolises the struggle facing all living beings and organisms of this world. But dare one wonder why that driving force is within all of us? What is it that makes us all want to survive and procreate, whatever our species? It must be there for some reason; if not it would be easier for all living organisms to capitulate and die. Why then should we struggle if there is nothing in that vast silent eternity to struggle for? But I guess that is a question that has troubled many far greater minds than my own over the centuries.

It is strange how throughout life one finds the unconscious ability to push back the terrible and the unpleasant almost out of one's mind and I realise that now, after over forty years, as I am writing it is perhaps the first time that I have been able to look at that event in my life logically and dispassionately.

From then on society busied itself with our affairs, led by a fat policeman who suggested that perhaps we had dropped the baby on his head without noticing. The funeral went by in a haze. We buried Paul in the tiny little churchyard at Leusdon, overlooking the beautiful Webburn valley that runs between it and its sister church at Buckland-in-the-Moor.

Gradually, as the numbness subsided, we began to throw ourselves into our work. I have always found that hard work is the best cure for most ailments, be they physical or mental. And after a year-and-a-half nature took its course and our second son Mark was born, again at Oldsbrim. By this time I had started a fencing business and with our small savings, and some borrowed capital, we managed to take a smallholding called West Cleave in the parish of Sourton on the northern edge of Dartmoor. Here our fencing business prospered and I managed to get contracts from two or three larger contractors (Mowlem Group) who were realigning the A30, the main arterial route to Cornwall. Within the first year we were employing four full-time men on the fence line erecting post and rail along the top of the batters beside the dual carriageway. I was making more money than I would have dreamed possible in the days of forestry and farming. Life seemed to be improving slightly, and we were able to pay off the loan at the end of that year, while also welcoming our third-born child, a daughter called Diane (Dee Dee for short), this time born at Okehampton hospital.

The elderly midwife was busy that night with a terrified teenager and on realising that I was a farmer she left me to deliver our new daughter into the world, tie off the umbilical cord, smack her bum and stand her on her head in the corner. I don't think she has ever forgiven me.

Of course over this period I was away from home for long hours and had the farm work to attend to when I got home, probably clocking up eighty hours a week or more, so consequently we didn't see very much of each other. I suppose in hindsight I was so ambitious to succeed I must have neglected my husbandly duties. The consequence of this folly was the eventual break-up of our marriage and this led, as these things usually do, to the enforced sale of the farm and business, also to the disappearance of my wife and family. Bless her, she actually ran off with a man called Tickle with a wooden leg! (That is if you can run with a wooden leg; perhaps hopped off would be a better term.) At that time I was completely devastated and certainly did not see the funny side of it. It was similar to the previous bereavement, but this time it was threefold; although looking back I guess the man probably did us both a favour. We were both very young and neither of us would have relished the path that the other chose through life.

So when the finances had been sorted I hightailed it back to the middle of Dartmoor and the place where I always felt safest. I lodged with my parents at Babeny for a while and rekindled my firewood and fencing business. The contract with the Mowlem Group had expired, so I concentrated on local agricultural fencing and helped my parents at home, although my father and I could never work together well. Coincidentally one of my fencing jobs was at Oldsbrim, which since I had left it had been sold to a young lady from the South Hams. We eventually became friends and started going out together. She had a mortgage on the property and my half of the sale of West Cleave was just enough to buy into a partnership with her.

Sarah was a hard-working and highly efficient farmer, having learned her trade as a farm labourer under Ken White at Broadhempston. She knew a great deal more about modern farming methods, silage making and so on, than I did. Conversely I knew a great deal more about farming on Dartmoor than her. Sarah was a perfectionist. Everything had to be just so, but unfortunately that trait in her character led her into fits of deep depression when things did not go quite according to plan. Nevertheless we made a good team and prospered, and within three or four years we managed to buy another small farm at Buckland-in-the-Moor.

Challamoor was a small grassy farm with common rights, although a trifle wet in places, and it was due to be sold at auction. Unfortunately the night before the auction the elderly couple who owned the farm (and were probably under great stress at having to sell up and leave) must have forgotten to check the open fire before going to bed. Fortunately no one was hurt, but the old house was burned to the ground. The auction took place the next day as planned, but the old couple were in an awful state and no one knew exactly what the legal situation was. With the uncertainty, the sale price was rather less than expected. We had the final nod and I think our gamble paid off. The next move was to sell the ruined farmhouse, and we were approached by a delightful couple from Landscove who had just sold a garden centre. They had great plans for the place and spent a lot of money doing it up in fine style. After selling the house we were left with the land at no cost and we farmed it in conjunction with Oldsbrim.

THE SPORT OF KINGS

'Mother would have nothing said against her beloved Arabs. I went the other way – the longer stride and the superior speed of the English blood horses made them rather special for me. My one overwhelming ambition was to own, train and ride one of my own…'

Clarence lungeing Rustum Bey with Freda up

FIRST STEPS

At that time my parents, and my mother particularly, had an Arab stallion at stud. He was called Rustum Bey and had been the equine alpha male for many years. Rustum had been used to cross with the local Dartmoor mares to produce children's ponies. The idea had been very successful and he had progeny all over Dartmoor and South Devon, but when he was nearing the end of his useful life they decided to buy a Thoroughbred mare for him to cover in the hope of producing an Anglo-Arab stallion to take over stud duties. Unfortunately the old boy was a bit past it – no equine Viagra in those days!

Fortunately Father had always maintained an interest in Thoroughbreds ever since my grandfather had bought a stallion from a man in Kingskerswell many years before. The vendor, by the name of Fogwell, had warranted the horse as sound and right in

86

every way and Father was sent down to ride it home. In those days twenty miles with quiet roads was no big deal and all went well for the first two. Unfortunately just as Father and horse were crossing the railway bridge at Newton Abbot a large flatulent steam train decided to belch its way underneath and, just for luck, gave a blast on its whistle. According to local taproom gossip the next eighteen miles – including Newton Abbot town centre – were covered in very short order.

The horse was called Strolling Vagabond, and it would not have taken much imagination to make him favourite at the next Buckfastleigh races. The Thoroughbred interest must have been genetic, although Mother would have nothing said against her beloved Arabs. I rather went the other way: the longer stride and the superior speed of the English blood horses made them rather special for me. My one overwhelming ambition was to own, train and ride one of my own. In the seventies it was still possible to win a point-to-point members' race with a good strong hunter, if it was fit enough and the going was heavy. Heavy, of course, was as often as much to the disadvantage of the amateur jockey as it was advantageous to the going. Unfortunately I fell into the former category. I needed to lose at least two stones.

I stood at 13 stone 3lb in my stockinged feet and had to be 11 stone 3lb in order to ride at 12 stone 7lb. My weight problem must have also been genetic as my paternal grandfather (who was incidentally a submariner in the Great War and the first able seaman to go out from Portsmouth in a submarine) left the Navy at 22 stone. How the hell he ever got in and out of the conning tower I know not, but that is another story. Anyway, after leaving the Navy he had to be reduced to 14 stone for health reasons and his diet was a simple one that I followed: stop sticking things in your mouth. It does actually work, so I lost my two stone and gained the racing bug.

My first job was to go out and find myself a useful point-to-pointer. I have always been of the view that the further west you go, the better the horses are, so having done some hunter trialling in the East Cornwall area, I took an evening off and went down to see an old acquaintance, Mr Thomas.

He was a dairy farmer and bred point-to-pointers very successfully as a hobby. I didn't know him well but I think to a small extent we shared the same dream. His best horse of that era was a little mare called Gay Coin. She had won several races for him, and although she was out of my reach financially she had a smaller sister, a four-year-old called Cornish Coin. She was a little mare not much over 15.2 hands, a kind of mousy bay with a kind eye and that incredible ability to shy at anything, including crisp packets and even blades of grass waving in the breeze. And when I say shy, that is no understatement. We could be jogging along on a quiet summer evening, quietly musing on nothing in particular, and in a split second we would the bolting down the road in the opposite direction with our eyes out on stalks and tail flailing in the wind like a startled ferret. This of course made life mildly interesting when we broke her in.

The little mare might not have had the legs or the height for really competitive racing but, bless her, she had the heart of a lion. We started long reining her in the traditional way as soon as we got her home. Not being used to Thoroughbreds we found her quite a handful to start with but she had a willing nature and wanted to learn, and when young horses, like young dogs, want to learn it is a joy to teach them. We had the few usual mishaps to start with, but once I had backed her we entered into a one-to-one relationship that I hope we both found satisfying. I certainly did.

For her first season most of my spare time went into her, taking her around the local countryside and doing a little hunting to get her the 'extra leg', that is to make her sure-

Jez on Davy Crockett (Rustum Bey x Mrs Tittlemouse), 1960

footed enough to both hunt over Dartmoor and jump 4-foot 3-inch fences at thirty miles an hour without going for a ball of chalk and taking me down with her. Even at that stage she was tremendously competitive, and when she was tired at the end of a hard day and facing a long hill in the wind and rain on the way home, she would lower her head and stick her little chin out. To feel the power in her hind quarters was a joy beyond compare.

> *And the swing of a blood horse striding*
> *On turf elastic and sound*
> *Is a joy secure and abiding,*
> *A kingship sceptred and crowned.*
> From 'A Handful of Leather' by William Henry Ogilvie (1869–1963)

Point-to-pointing, of course, was an old tradition in the countryside. It had almost died out and was apparently rejuvenated at Sherborne around 1880. The original idea was to get from one point to another across country, and often back again, faster than your rivals, jumping or negotiating any obstacles that happened to be in the way. Of course the local man on the home-bred hunter who knew his country well usually had the advantage. I would imagine it possibly started as a light-hearted and perhaps an inebriated pastime after the end of the hunting season. It must have been a dangerous one for anyone who did not know the lie of the land, with horses often breaking legs or being bogged in a strange country. This type of racing presumably moved on to a race between two church spires or steeples (hence the term steeplechasing). Gradually as the sport progressed, and more horses and riders were killed, the fences were made safer and more regular.

It was necessary to exclude tricks like the one allegedly played by one Tom Oliver, who apparently on a foggy day completed one circuit and hid himself and his horse behind a hayrick, joining in again on the third and going on to win. This would not be possible now in a modern point-to-point which is generally run over a two-and-a-half to three-mile course, often involving nineteen or twenty fences, usually within sight of the crowd. Just imagine taking nineteen or twenty fences standing 4 feet 3 inches at thirty miles an hour over approximately six minutes. The adrenalin rush is enough to make anyone's tail stand on end. I remember explaining this to old Gillian Howard one day and adding that 'it was better than sex'. On that occasion Gillian fixed me with her steely stare, exclaiming: 'You must have met some bloody dull women in your day, boy!' But as I get older, I think perhaps I was right!

Once little Cornish Coin was backed and going regularly, and I considered her to

Babeny, on the bridlepath leading to the East Dart river, 2016

be hunting fit, I started her in serious training for the lower echelons of the sport of kings. Hunting fit in those days was considerably fitter than most of today's hunters, hacks and hirelings. In Father's generation the South Devon Hunt was kennelled at Barton Pines near Paignton on the coast and their furthest meet was at the Warren House Inn above Postbridge on the high moor, a distance of some twenty miles. The horses were 'sent on' from Paignton well before first light, with grooms riding and leading, to arrive at the meet by eleven o'clock ready for the masters and huntsman to commence the day's hunting. After four to eight hours' hard hunting on the high moor the grooms would hack them back to kennels. This of course was an exceptional day. Imagine the delicate young owners of today throwing up their hands in horror at that sort of regime for their beloved and often over-pampered mounts, most of them thinking quite sincerely that two hours' exercise twice a week is more than the average hack can handle.

Over the weeks and months little Coin pounded the roads and tracks around the Poundsgate, Postbridge and Dartmeet area, gradually becoming lean and limber; starting at daylight six mornings a week, for two-and-a-half hours, only walking for the first few weeks, gradually building up to trotting, which is the most useful pace for getting a horse fit and developing respiration. When we could trot up the road from Newbridge through Poundsgate to the top of Sherill Hill without sweating, then and only then would we both be fit enough to move on to faster work.

Of course galloping around the grass fields during a wet winter was not an option, so at a farm sale I purchased an old grass cutting machine for a couple of pounds and cut a quarter-mile circular track in the heather on Riddon Ridge, and a kindly neighbour over at Stadiscombe Farm near Holne, called Arthur Brown, allowed me to cut bundles of birch in his woodland around Gallant le Bower. This we bound tightly and transported back to Babeny. Combined with some not-too-stout ash poles it made two quite passable steeplechase fences, and by galloping this circuit four times I gave myself two miles and eight fences. This of course only came in at the very end of her training, but was by far the most exciting part.

As in most sports, the early and intermediate stages of training are the most important and a slow hard slog reaps dividends. It is always important to keep the horse up in his paces. Years ago there were two small racing yards in a local town and I had to travel through the area to collect an employee in the early mornings. On my way out I would usually meet the horses in training at one stable coming home at a brisk pace after exercise, with the lads and lasses a'top chatting cheerfully and enjoying their work. On my way back I would meet the second stable string slouching out after morning stables with grumpy dour faces on both horses and riders, the riders usually sporting a half-smoked cigarette and an expression that signified they wished they were elsewhere. It doesn't need to be said that the first stable owner-trainer went on to many successes, including getting the leg up on the winner of the Grand National.

Riding over 'chase fences is perhaps not quite as dangerous as it looks. At racing speed the jumps come quite easily with a low trajectory and, if a mistake is made and fall suffered, usually you are thrown well clear of the horse. You very soon learn to roll up into a small ball and wait until the thunder of hooves and flying scads has passed, and then perhaps open one eye at a time. It is definitely not wise to spring to your feet to reassure the onlookers that you are okay, and then get knocked 'arse over breakfast' by a back-marker. The far more dangerous sport is eventing, 'a game for brave men's playing'. The pace is slower, the jumps are solid and unforgiving, and often the steep drops after a jump mean that if the horse falls it is quite likely to fall on top of you, and half a ton of horse falling on you from a great height is no joke.

But my first and real love was always steeplechasing, and so smitten was I that I took on a grey mare, Princess Pamina, from her owner (Briony Kennard) to train alongside little Cornish Coin. Pamina was a bigger mare with a lot more bone, and although they were both novices the fact that they were jumping side by side gave them both a little more courage and competitive edge.

FIRST RACE

Eventually came the day of my first race. The chosen venue was at Forches Cross near Newton Abbot. It was a beautiful spring day, a blue sky peppered with fluffy white clouds, flags bravely fluttering in the breeze and, much to my consternation, a very large crowd, many of whom were local friends and neighbours. I had dressed myself carefully in my racing colours which were an old black T-shirt with a red horse bandage stitched around the middle, a pair of very light nylon breeches with a blue stripe (lent to me by Dennis Ferrens MFH) and worn over a pair of nylon tights stolen from a local stable girl. The tights were actually quite warm and obviously very light, and they had the added advantage of keeping my wedding-tackle out of harm's way.

While the horses were being led around the paddock, feeling slightly self-conscious I sauntered over to the doorway of the beer tent to talk to some neighbouring farmers. While we were in conversation about the state of the going, the weather, the opposition and so on, a local acquaintance very generously (and I believe quite harmlessly) came out of the beer tent and thrust a large glass of whisky into my hand. Just at that moment Dennis Ferrens, 'hero', Master of Foxhounds and accomplished amateur jockey, strode into sight. He treated both me and the tumbler of whisky to a long withering stare, turned on his heel and strode away. To this day I honestly believe that he thought I did not have the balls to ride without the whisky! If there were ever a few seconds in a lifetime when I would like to have turned back the clock, it was then. The damage was done and explanations would have been futile, and only made matters worse.

I was legged up on Pamina and we cantered down to the start. There were fourteen or fifteen runners in the race and we all circled slowly while the starter's assistant tightened girths and so on. The mare had been young, slab-sided and ungainly when she came to me a couple of months before, but now she had a good shine on her coat and she felt firm-muscled and well-balanced under me. As we circled she played happily with her bit, showing off to the other runners in the happy naïveté of a novice before her first race, which brings me neatly to a minor point about the integrity of racing – a point that I have always found rather interesting! Many owners and trainers, when sending a novice horse out to run for the first time, like the horse to have an enjoyable experience: to lie up well covered in the middle of the field and not be hassled or stretched too far, working on the theory that the first experience should always be a good one, and they instruct their jockeys accordingly. This of course is a reasonable practice from the point of view of the horse, but not quite fair on the elderly pensioner who has taken a shine to the horse in the paddock and laid half a week's pension on the horse's nose. But of course you can't please both the pensioner and the horse, which gives an interesting slant on the term 'pulling a race' – training or cheating?

Anyway, a novice on a novice is never an ideal marriage, and being young and inexperienced my plan was at least to see if I could get around. The first fence is always wider than the rest, giving everyone a fair chance of daylight. We hit it in line abreast with stirrup irons clashing and bits of birch flying in the breeze. From then on as the race settled down I lay up a handy fourth or fifth, being careful to allow daylight in front of her nose so that she could see to jump clearly, always keeping a keen eye on the horse and rider in front, knowing that if they disappeared over the fence and did not appear again you had to veer off for fear of landing on top of a heap of thrashing legs and arms.

Nearing the end of the second circuit I was still lying up quite handy and looking almost dangerous. The danger, of course, was soon noted by a more experienced jockey who quickly pulled up beside me, stealing my ground and half-lengthing me. This is an old trick that often works on young novice horses. The plan is to pull up beside the youngster, and while not actually interfering with him you try to break his stride pattern and generally fluster him until immediately before the next fence when you pull half a length ahead and consequently take off half a length in advance. The desired result, if achieved, means that the confused youngster leaves the ground at the same time as you, half a length too soon. On this occasion the trick worked perfectly. Pamina and I landed four square in the centre of the fence at thirty miles an hour. Fortunately I rolled four or five yards in advance, spitting out mouthfuls of grass and blood. I had only bitten my tongue, although at the time I felt half murdered and very badly used.

That day I not only learnt a little about myself and a little about other jockeys, but also a little about owners. My own strode determinedly after her horse, which I guess was fair enough, but throughout the rest of the afternoon she equally determinedly avoided asking after my health. When we met in the beer tent later on for a post-race analysis, she dutifully offered me a drink. Pulling my forelock in the time-honoured way I replied, 'Thank you kindly, ma'am, I will take half a lager.' To my amusement when I returned the compliment a little while later she insisted on a double brandy and lovage! God bless her. One must remember that young jockeys are two a penny, but a good horse is always worth looking after.

CHARACTERS HUMAN...

Racing and its peripheral areas of support have a habit of throwing up wonderful characters, one such being an old neighbour of mine, one Peggy Booty. Peggy had spent a great deal of her youth on and around Exmoor and had been a supporter of the Devon and Somerset Staghounds. She presumably also had connections with the flat racing fraternity, and I remember sitting with her late one night in her old thatched Dartmoor longhouse at Sherrill. It was a typical Dartmoor winter night with 'beeches dripping in browns and duns', and 'threshing and plying' (from 'Weathers' by Thomas Hardy) in a wind that seemed to come straight in from Alaska, but we were sharing a nice bottle of malt Scotch and her face lit up with the glow of the open fire as she related a wonderful tale of racing days. I say 'tale' advisedly, as to this day I have not got a clue if it was the truth or just a great yarn.

Apparently in her youth she had mixed with the young and beautiful of the day including the famous flat race jockey, Steve Donoghue. At the time of the yarn, Peggy must have been an octogenarian, or at least knocking on the door, but her memory of the day that Steve Donoghue won the Derby was as clear as if it had happened yesterday. On the evening of Derby day, Donoghue held a large victory party. Apparently the hotel was packed to the rafters with the rich and famous, and the owner of the winner had commissioned a glass blower to make twelve stem glasses with a large bubble blown into each stem showing a horse and jockey inside wearing the colours of the owner. During the party these were presented to Steve Donoghue, whereupon the most famous jockey of the decade escorted Peggy Booty from the crowd round the dance floor and, one by one, he hurled the commemorative glasses into the fireplace, all but the last one, and going down on bended knee in front of the assembled company he presented it to Peggy! The old face became beautiful with the memory, and who the hell cares if it was the truth or not. The glass stands in my cabinet to this day, and occasionally I look at it with a grin and remember the old girl.

In those far-off racing days another amazing character comes to mind, a man with no knowledge of horses or horsemanship apart from occasional visits to the bookmaker, Ron Honeysett. Ron was a self-made jewellery dealer from the East End of London and a part-time pawnbroker. I can't remember exactly how he came into life at Babeny, but we taught him to ride and he immediately caught the bug. He was possessed of a string of jewellery and pawnshops and a gigantic ego. Anything that Ron wanted he had – there were no half measures in his life – and I remember one day he decided to take us all to the Cheltenham Festival. We were duly loaded into his large BMW and whisked off in the general direction of Cheltenham. At that time I had a great deal of work to do, but Ron was not to be denied.

En route, he decided to stop for an early lunch or late breakfast at a small country pub. Apparently the landlord was expecting a large party for lunch and couldn't accommodate us. This wouldn't do for Ron. He placed a paternal arm around the landlord's shoulder, asking him quite forcibly how much he would make from the expected lunch party and telling him to cancel them so that we could have the pub to ourselves, and of course Ron would make up the loss and bung him a ton on top. Progressing on the same theme we arrived at Cheltenham only to discover a long and tedious traffic jam. Ron, not being in the habit of waiting, and much to the embarrassment of the rest of us, drove his large BMW smack into the middle of a beautifully manicured lawn. When the poor owner came spluttering out to protest he had £500 thrust into his top pocket and was left to consider the morality of the situation along with four tyre marks.

Feud won the Adjacent Hunts Open at Eggesford Point-to-Point in March 1982; (*front row left to right*) Jez, unknown, Sarah, Gilly Smith (holding Feud) and jockey Darkie Ellis PHOTOGRAPH © EXPRESS & ECHO

... AND EQUINE

But extraordinary characters wax and wane very quickly in racing, and poor Princess Pamina's star very quickly waned. She was ever a good hunter but lacked the fire and aggression that would serve her well in the racing field. So from then on all my time and effort was put at the disposal of little Cornish Coin. She definitely had what it took, as did her mother and grandmother, bless her. I can always remember the quaint way she had of standing and peering over her shoulder at you. She was a courageous little lady and nothing upset her more than another horse trying to overtake her. She had by this time become well used to schooling over fences in the company of other horses, and although she looked rather small and insignificant she was hard racing fit, with a season's hunting behind her. And with the coming of the next point-to-point season we entered her for her first race.

After due consideration we placed her in a novice point-to-point race at Flete Park run by the Dartmoor Foxhounds. The going was good, soft in places, and for her first outing, following the golden rule of not putting a novice on a novice, I asked a friend of mine, Darkie Ellis – who was considerably more experienced – to take the ride.

Darkie knew her well and came up to Babeny to school her over fences. His instructions for the day were to keep well out of trouble but in touch with the leaders until he got to the top of the hill on the last circuit, then if he felt he was in with a chance to kick on and down the hill. You can often make up a great deal of ground going downhill without taking too much out of the horse. The first part of the plan worked beautifully, the second part worked even better; the little mare had picked up three or four places going down the hill and disappeared into the dip lying up third.

For half a minute my heart refused to beat and I refused to breathe. The sight of our black and red colours following the little mare's ears going up over the last fence in the lead closed down my whole cardiovascular system completely. I felt elated, nauseous and dizzy all at the same time, so much so that I almost forgot to collect my winnings – all of £20. The little mare had done us proud, coming in handsomely at 20 to 1. The fact that it had cost £40 to enter, along with the transport, wages and so on, didn't enter into the scheme of things.

The mare then went on to further modest success, and feeling rather proud of myself I immediately hightailed it up to Ascot for the autumn sales. Lurking in the dark recesses of one of the boxes was a large brown gelding. He had a speculative but rather sour look in his eye, plenty of bone and heart room, and on trotting him up I found he had a magnificent stride. He was perhaps slightly past his sell-by-date – I think he was twelve – but his form showed that he had been a good horse in his day, and early in his career had won a couple of good steeplechases over three miles on heavy going. He had come from a big yard, and sometimes in a big busy yard older horses can't be afforded the individual attention that can occasionally pull a little more from them. Often, if they are made to feel special on a one-to-one basis, they will give a little more and save a little less.

Feud was a perfect gentleman and schoolmaster. He wore the T-shirt of experience with a combination of pride and resignation. He was kind and considerate in the box and to take a steeplechase fence at speed seemed nothing more than just an extra stride, but he was a little sour and tired of racing, and only put in as much effort as he considered strictly necessary.

After a few days I turned the old boy out in a field with some pretty young teenage fillies for company. It was good to see him initially relax, then become paternally dominant and eventually ease himself into the role of alpha male. For the first time in his life he was living a semi-natural herd-oriented life. His mindset completely changed, he arranged the younger horses in strict pecking order, spent long hours gazing across the valley (presumably in search of predators) and even started his own personal dung pile at the top corner of the field, marking the end of his territory.

The next step was to take him hunting; as far as I could ascertain he had never hunted before. As with most horses his first day out was almost a non-event. His ears held a permanent question mark and for most of the day he pottered around vaguely, searching for the training gallop and wondering what all the noise was about. But by the afternoon he was getting the hang of it. Like most of the field, both four-legged and two, he neither saw nor cared much about the fox, but galloping happily about after twenty-two couple of noisy hounds suited his new image as herd leader, and although the rough country was new to him he strained every sinew to stay in front. The old spirit gradually returned and a week later, on his second day's hunting, he left his little herd of fillies with a stern warning as to their behaviour and strode into the field like an experienced and seasoned warrior. This, of course, was as I had hoped ,and two weeks later I entered him into the Adjacent Hunts race at Eggesford.

The going was exceptionally heavy and as he was an unknown quantity, the bookmakers had him at 50 to 1, and so did I. The old man had fire in his loins again. He pulled on through the mud like a plough horse and left a good field of sixteen in his wake. Like many another middle-aged gent, a little flirtation and hunting had sharpened him up considerably.

The locals had a strong favourite of their own for that race and there were a few long faces in the beer tent. We didn't dwell on our going and loaded up as soon as was decent and headed back for Dartmoor.

The next adventure in the sport of kings involved a nice little bay horse called

Benghazi Express. I bought him, again quite cheaply at Ascot, from Jenny Pitman. He was an honest little horse and a week later I rode him to a creditable third in a big field at Lamalla, near Liskeard. That is, creditable from his point of view, for I think perhaps he was placed in spite of me. At that time I was not riding well as I had for some time been having trouble with my peripheral vision and my balance.

Jez and Benghazi Express

SERIOUS SETBACK

I had been to see the local medic on several occasions over a period of six months with a selection of wonderfully strange symptoms. I had blacked out several times in the yard, my balance was impaired and I was developing tunnel vision. Unfortunately for both of us, my father had suffered from migraine, the knowledge of which manifested itself in a chronic case of medical 'tunnel vision'. I returned to the surgery time after time presenting worsening symptoms and after many more months I felt like a scrounger at the wrong end of the dole queue, trying to demand a sick note. I was of course self-employed and had never claimed any benefit of any sort in my life, and the last thing I wanted was to take time off work. I can well remember my last visit to my GP. I stumbled clumsily into his surgery to be greeted with the comment: 'Not you again! You are overstressed, overworked and you will just have to live with it, there is nothing we can do!'

At that stage, in sheer desperation I joined a private health scheme. After all, it was easy: 'There was nothing wrong with me!' Under the scheme I persuaded my GP to refer me to a consultant neurologist at Exeter, and this renowned and rather stuffy gentlemen subjected me to a great many tests, encephalographs and the like. Peering at me over an antique dealer's dream of fine porcelain set on a green velvet tablecloth, he pronounced in an icy voice that would not be denied: 'Overstressed, overworked and hereditary migraine.' I returned a little shaken to my world of blackouts, visual problems and a slight gnawing fear in my gut. After all, great men of medicine must be right, because they say so.

I continued stumbling downhill both mentally and physically for several more months until I plucked up enough courage to go back to my GP. On hearing the same story for the umpteenth time he gave a slight shrug of the shoulders and exclaimed, 'As you're obviously not satisfied, I am sending you to a friend of mine in Torquay who is a psychiatrist.' My explosive comment of 'why should I need a bloody psychiatrist?' was fortunately not heeded.

The psychiatrist was actually quite a nice guy (as they have to be), and after a deep and meaningful discussion on fuchsias and fishing he very kindly offered me a cup of tea. When the equally nice nurse arrived with the tea she dropped anchor on my port side. For a moment I didn't realise that she was there until she coughed very politely. I jumped and the tea went all over the floor. The psychiatrist, putting five and five together and making ten, unlike his colleagues, suggested that I went straight in for a CAT scan. Now being a fully paid-up member of a private health plan I was whisked into hospital in 48 hours.

It was a couple of weeks before I heard from my GP, by which time I had convinced myself that as no one wanted to see me I was probably okay. On my arrival at surgery I was greeted by a worried-looking practitioner, who informed me that the CAT scan had shown up a large cerebral tumour. As it was the size of a small apple I would have to go back for more tests, but it might be a good idea if I was to get all my affairs in order. I suppose if there is one phrase in the English language that is guaranteed to scare the crap out of someone that is probably it.

The fear was almost physical, as if I had been kicked in the pit of the guts by a blood horse. I am not lucky enough to have religion, and as the cold claws of fear spread through me I remember feeling very small and very alone. For many nights I slept little, if at all, and I remember one night following the tradition of most animals that feel they have come to the end of their particular road: I walked through the night back to Laughter. It was a fine clear night and I spent a couple of hours sitting under 'her, my Rowan tree', gazing up at eternity. Someone said there are as many heavenly bodies around us as there are grains of sand on all the beaches of the entire world. That night, looking out into time and space, I could well believe it. Perhaps as great a fear as that of the unknown was the fear of losing control of my own destiny. There was still so much left to do, and I had no intention of leaving it undone.

I didn't realise it at the time, but apparently three local churches had offered up a small prayer for me at their Sunday service. Perhaps those six parishioners just swung the balance! And after all, when the sun looked above the horizon he would see the heather and the gorse in bloom, and they say kissing is in season when the gorse is in bloom and the gorse is always in bloom somewhere, so the Grim Reaper would just have to wait.

At least in the great conflicts of the world a man had a chance to fight back. Surely the heat and turmoil of battle must be preferable to this cold insidious disease killing from within. I hadn't had the chance to fight, but I had no intention of joining the cream of the last generation. I could see them in my mind's eye, friendly old faces with a dry humour, pipes clenched between their teeth, gnarled old knuckles grasping blackthorn sticks, Peter, Joe and Owen, with Whiff and Jack, all the Frenches,

'I could see them in my mind's eye...' – locals in the Tavistock Inn, Poundsgate, 1950s: landlady Maud (white shirt, fifth from left); Johnny French (cap, centre back)

and bow-legged Sid Beard with his cows strolling bravely along the great black highway to infinity, big characters all of them, as familiar and comforting as a well-thumbed and often read favourite book. But they had at least had the chance to serve their time on this mortal coil. No! As I was wheeled on my back down the great white floodlit highway to theatre, I resolved to put off renewing my acquaintance with them for as long as possible.

The surgeon was a nice guy called Strachan (he must have been a nice guy because he was a sea trout fishermen). I remember thinking that if his hand was steady enough to tie a small fly on a gossamer thread neatly enough to fool a sea trout, perhaps I stood a chance. The operation lasted for about six hours and it involved cutting the top of my head off like a boiled egg. The anaesthetist (who was also a sea trout fisherman) told me that they used a Black and Decker (and sea trout fishermen, unlike salmon fishermen, don't lie). During the operation I remember having a strange experience, hardly an out-of-body experience or even a peep into the afterlife. I remember quite clearly regaining semi-consciousness while a nurse was busily wiping my backside. When I related this to the anaesthetist later he turned a whiter shade of pale and hastily explained that in modern medicine it is preferable to keep a patient as close to consciousness as possible. But I could not conceivably have regained my wits: perhaps I just have a vivid imagination? I remained in intensive care for about a week with two nurses sleeping one each side of me, or at least taking it in turns to sleep. Fortunately I was kept full of morphine, but even so my pillow felt like a bag of bricks.

As soon as I escaped from intensive care – and against medical advice – I crammed a balaclava over my shaven head and hired a taxi once a day to take me back to look after the stock. That was the best therapy I could have had. Convalescence was as short as I could make it. Physically I was not in bad shape, but for several weeks my brain played tricks on me. Occasionally I would watch people going about their daily business while their legs appeared to be walking backwards: very confusing. Even the seagulls flew backwards! My short-term memory was badly affected, and to an extent my capacity for recognition. Although I maintained the memory of my surroundings and my existence within them, the comfort of familiarity was completely gone.

My family and people that I knew well appeared as strangers, the dogs and horses, even familiar hedgerows and fields that I had often ploughed and trimmed appeared strange and threatening. I suppose on the lighter side my lack of recognition made me feel as if I was bedding a different woman every night, but that was a problem with which I did not burden my wife! It took the medics nearly a week to inform me that the tumour was benign. I felt that this was rather thoughtless and when I eventually plucked up enough courage to ask, they told me that they assumed I had already guessed. On my release I took up more exercise, first walking many miles a day and then I progressed to jogging. I am still not sure whether I wanted to rid my body of the disease through exercise or if I was running away from the fear and the stress. Anyway, I got fit enough to ride in a point-to-point within six weeks. It was good to be alive again. There was a shine on my Rowan leaves, a crystal twinkle on my river! Atheist or otherwise, I sent up a small prayer of thanks just in case anyone was listening.

One always hopes that in extreme adversity one can pull something positive from the experience. My positive was the realisation that life is a very short road and that one must pull sixty seconds out of every minute, sixty minutes out of every hour, and that working with the supposition that on average we spend twenty years of our life unconscious, time spent sleeping is time wasted: a robbery from the great gift of life.

IRISH HORSE FAIR

At this time I was still very much into hunting and racing. Having enjoyed most of Somerville and Ross, *Some Experiences of an Irish RM* and the rest – all set in southern Ireland around the County Cork area – my imagination fell in love with the people, animals and traditions of that time, perhaps because the west coast of Ireland thirty-five years ago was similar to the small insular, rural community of my childhood. They were both vanishing cultures, grimly clinging to inherited lifestyles, blissfully unaware of the tsunami of bureaucratic change that would sweep them away forever.

At the time my wife Sarah was suffering from a bout of clinical depression, probably brought on by the strain of dealing with my temporary infirmity. So on little more than a whim we took passage from Holyhead on the wild Irish Sea – at least my grandfather used to say it was the roughest sea in the world. Fortunately on that particular day it was as calm as a millpond, and after a couple of hours or so we nosed our way gently through the screaming gulls into Rosslare Harbour. What with the calm sea and half-price Paddy whiskey, my first experience as a sailor was a good one.

We were travelling in a small Renault 5, rather conspicuous in Tory blue with English plates. Ireland was at the height of its 'troubles' and perhaps we would have been wiser to hire a car. Anyway we cut across country towards Limerick, partly because our local MFH had arranged an appointment with Hugh Robard, the Master of the Limerick, and partly because we were to meet one of Ireland's more famous horse dealers, Mr Michael Leonard. At the time the exchange rate between the punt and the pound was quite favourable, and we had high hopes of buying a horse of some quality.

On our first night we stayed in a small farmhouse B&B just outside Limerick. Looking out over the lush green countryside it was easy to see why Ireland is known as the Emerald Isle. Most of the livestock, including the horses, were in beautiful condition, grazing on the strangely level and lush pasture, bathed in the warm moist air swinging in off the Atlantic and the Gulf Stream. I had always assumed that most of Ireland was rocky and mountainous, but there are many thousands of acres of gently rolling grassland and I assume that a proportion of it must be on limestone. At any rate, they breed fine horses with good feet and hard bone.

Limerick in those days was quite a hot bed of unrest. The provisional IRA were active in the area and although the elderly owners of the B&B were courteous and friendly, most of the walls of the house were liberally sprinkled with photographs of local martyrs gunned down or imprisoned by the English.

We had stayed with the old couple for a few days and had spent most of our time drinking Guinness and being ushered around the local fields by old nagsmen and horse dealers who assumed that as we had come from England we were inexperienced, rich and not too bright. We had paraded before us a long string of dodgy, vaguely dodgy and three-legged hopefuls. It took them nearly to the end of the week to realise that we weren't really English; we were just moorland peasant farming stock much like their own hillbillies that occasionally wandered in from the coast to barter a couple of pigs and a donkey for a rough cart cob. One old boy came wandering up the road with his nag in the evening light (which is always useful if you don't want a man to see a horse too well). They hobbled up to the door and I wasn't sure which of them was the worse for the corns, the man or the horse. On being asked if the horse could jump the old boy fixed me with a beady eye and hobbled off into a boggy field. Scrambling up onto a five-foot hedge with a long lunging rein and a hunting whip, he proceeded to canter the old horse around one field, over the hedge on which he stood, around the field behind him and back over the hedge again. He was right. The old horse could jump, despite all his unsoundnesses and a minor discrepancy between his two shoes, with one leg the size and consistency of a gatepost, and barbed wire both sides of the hedge.

It was not long before they realised we weren't quite the colour of the shamrock. The light of avarice paled in their eyes and we all got down to a good session of Guinness drinking and tall-tale telling. It was in a bar in Limerick that a dear old boy by name of Ron Donovan gave me probably the best bit of advice I have ever had in my life. In a wonderful Irish brogue he advised me, very paternally and very carefully, that 'throughout the rest of my life I should endeavour to keep my belly button as far away from my backbone as possible and never to have anything to do with bloody lawyers'. Not a bad piece of advice after twelve pints of Guinness.

Anyway, after the fun and jollification was over we bought a very large round and moved on to the establishment of Mr Michael Leonard who was a horse dealer of some repute (and hopefully drank less Guinness). Michael's was a beautiful and substantial yard, populated by a great many beautiful and substantial horses. The man had done his homework. Over a couple of days we were presented with two or three suitable horses. There was no pressure and we were given time to think (which is always a good policy if you are not sure of your horses). One young chestnut mare stood out above the others, not particularly in stature but definitely in character. Her sire was Carnival Night, a great jumping sire of his time (or 'a grand lepper' to put it in the vernacular). She had obviously inherited her father's jumping ability and, in a rash moment, I tried her over a five-barred gate. The experience was close to riding a missile up and being kicked downstairs all at once. Fortunately the gate stayed in position and so did I. The next day, much to my gratification, I was allowed to take her out around the leafy lanes of southern Ireland without an escort.

In that area the hedgerows were devoid of mature timber but were heavily populated with the most wonderful summer flowers, particularly pink campion was everywhere. After a mile or two of solitude and greenery laced with tranquillity, I was happy in the knowledge that in such a pastoral and rural setting nothing could possibly grate on the nerves of a young and flighty filly. But suddenly both the young mare and I were considerably alarmed, while negotiating a sharp bend in the road, to come face to face with a large metal ball, of similar size to your average cannon ball, bouncing down the road towards us at twenty-five to thirty miles per hour, hotly pursued by twenty-five to thirty couple of bouncing, miscellaneous and presumably indigenous Irish madmen in full cry. The troop was led by half a dozen scruffy urchins on bicycles closely followed by the late teen to early thirties generation, trailed by their fathers and uncles accompanied by various tradesmen, who in turn were hustled along by two purple-faced bookmakers and a clerk.

Apparently it is popular in that part of Ireland to charge along the highways and byways in pursuit of a metal ball and wager on how far it will travel at each throw, unfortunately not preceded by a gentleman with a red flag. Anyway, the whole scenario was rather too much for the young horse and its uneducated rider. Gilded Gamble, as we decided to call her, spun on a sixpence and with jaws as wide open as would do credit to any crocodile she hightailed it back to her owner's yard. Not being quite sure of the state of play I was very happy to go with her, at least most of the way. In the final furlong the silly bitch espied a conveniently large horse transporter 'with its mouth wide open' and bolted straight up the ramp with me still in the plate, and stood quivering in its darkest recesses. The amusement it afforded the staff was hard to bear, capped only by Michael strolling over and suggesting that if I was that keen to buy, perhaps I should pay for her before loading. Only a true Irishman can turn disaster to advantage with that quick humour.

After enjoying B&B plus evening meal for a few days in the small guesthouse, and thinking to give our hosts an evening off, we decided without recommendation to take supper in the local village. You will remember we were driving a small car with English plates and following hospitalisation, shaven head and so on, my hair was still very short (army style). A few miles up the road we came across a village hall. From the car park the place looked well lit and very jolly. Sounds of great mirth and merriment issued from within and flooded across the countryside. Thinking in our naïveté that it might be nice to witness a local Irish dance and perhaps get something to eat, we entered and strolled up to the bar. First the conversation died, then the music stopped. You could have heard the proverbial pin drop. The little bit of hair I had left on the back of my neck stood on end and I felt about as comfortable as a rat in a barrel.

With a mumbled apology that included words like 'good evening', 'sorry', 'wrong place' we retraced our steps back to the car (which fortunately still had its wheels on), and drove hastily back to the B&B. We learned later that the pet name for Limerick among the Dublin taxi drivers is Stab City! Why? We knew not, but we had learned our lesson and decided from then on to stay in our comfort zone.

So looking through the paper that evening we spied a horse sale a few miles away in the direction of County Kerry (horse dealers versus 'shinners', no contest). Bright and early next morning, donning our oldest clothes (including a very old slouch hat for me), away we drove for about an hour. Eventually after much benign misdirection in a language that we could barely understand, we arrived at a muddy field of approximately five acres, crowded with all the many delights of an Irish horse fair. There were rural interests of every description, ranging from fat old feathery Shire horses all the way down to donkeys, geese, ferrets and more. There were tinkers selling a myriad of wares, tower blocks of small caged birds and a dear ragged old lady covered in gold selling crystal balls from the boot of a Bentley. We were particularly amused by two small children, probably siblings, aged by their teeth at between five and seven years, sitting cross-legged on a blanket selling cheap watches. Being at that time in the want of a watch and being charmed by the sweet cherubic faces, I examined one of the watches fairly carefully and inquired of the young gentleman if it was likely to keep good time. Obviously frustrated by my pedantic English ways he fixed me with a gimlet eye and growled: 'If you want to buy a bloody watch, mister, buy one. If not, move along. We're damned busy.' So much for Irish cherubs.

Of course the main business of the day was the sale of hunters, hacks, racing trotters, pacers and cobs of every description. Most of the horses were run up and down the street, as fast as possible, with the occasional cat and the odd hen fleeing into the margin of the crowd to escape the mud and flying hooves, while the horse handlers screeching something in old Irish which sounded like 'for-a-balla' or even 'faugh-baller' (it obviously meant 'keep out of the bloody way'), ran until their faces turned purple and the Guinness sweated from them wet enough to stick the shirts to their backs.

Most of the horses had lately been languishing in 'green pastures the quiet waters by', and after marinating themselves in the peace and tranquillity of the Irish countryside they were not unnaturally a trifle alarmed at the hustle and bustle of the fair field. As is always the case with rustic youngsters, the alarm manifested itself in several different and interesting ways.

One particular bright bay colt standing a good 16 hands to the wither with mane in dreadlocks and a wedge of forelock firmly matted together with sticky burdock burrs took great exception to the general hubbub, and with eyes out on stalks charged valiantly at a small inoffensive donkey cart with two first-class pigs as passengers. Changing feet expertly on what appeared to be the pigs' heads he disappeared into the crowd, only to reappear an instant later in full and fast reverse having plunged his front leg up to the knee through the frame of a red and black perambulator (fortunately empty). Presumably then realising that he had passed beyond his level of personal experience, he stood rooted to the ground on three legs holding the offending article out in front of him until someone kindly removed it. Only a good Catholic horse, used to a multitude of children, could get away with that. In England it would have been a major disaster with screaming women, crying children and a multitude of heavy vets' bills, to say nothing of one insurance claim, two health and safety officials, three paramedics, four fat policemen, five pompous stewards and a ban on next year's fair.

As we proceeded on our leisurely way to the bottom of the field (far from the Garda who were sensibly investigating a clearish liquid in an old lemonade bottle at the top), we happened on a sizeable crowd all cheering and waving coats and hats. Not being tall enough to see what was presumably a horse of some considerable quality, I shouldered my way to the front.

Once I'd got to the front of the jostling crowd (not for the first time in Ireland I wondered if I was perhaps in the right place at the wrong time, or even just the wrong place), the crowd had formed a circle. In the centre space were two men stripped to the waist, heavily built, hard of muscle, both with the dark handsome hollow-eyed look of their Celtic ancestors, perhaps mixed with a little Spanish blood, or even French (for history has it that during the rebellion of 1798 a French fleet sailed into Bantry Bay, but was dispersed by a great storm and possibly also a Mass offered up by the local priest and his flock, and who knows how many lusty young French sailors swam ashore and abandoned Napoleon for a soft Irish breast?).

As I watched, the shorter of the two swung a vicious bare-knuckle right hook into the small ribs of his opponent; the blow landed with the hollow thud of a bullet hitting flesh. His taller adversary countered with a flashing left cross that peeled and puckered the flesh from a prominent eyebrow. Both men were bleeding heavily from various cuts and abrasions; the blood had trickled down their heaving chests and congealed in the black matted hair. It was not difficult to imagine the salt taste of the blood and the sweat stinging in the eyes. There seemed to be no animosity in the way they looked at each other, just a grim determination not to be beaten. The match continued for some ten to fifteen minutes with some skilful punching and counterpunching. Both men had obviously lost their pugilistic virginity long before and each punch was delivered with full body weight behind it, but eventually exhaustion started to set in and the level of skill dropped until one wild haymaker that started from the knees felled the larger man. When it was eventually agreed that he could not rise unaided, the victor grasped his hand and pulled him to his feet, clapping him on the back. They left together for the beer tent and a gallon of porter each.

It later transpired that the bare-knuckle fighters had no dispute between themselves, but some weeks before there had been a wedding between their two families and an old grudge had fermented with the alcohol. As often happens in these cases, the eminently reasonable decision was made by the heads of the families that instead of turning the wedding into a bloodbath, they would each produce the best fighter of the family for a contest at the next horse fair. Perhaps some politicians of the world should take note. This rather civilised (Old Testament) way of settling a score differs of course from the more professional pugilism (in quieter fields!) where a line of contenders stand to be inspected by the champion, who stalks up and down the line staring hard into the eyes of each contender and eventually touching one on the shoulder. The rest is not for the imagination of the fainthearted.

Having eventually regained our lodgings, we retired for an early night. After all, Dublin cabbies should know something about Ireland.

Bright and early the next morning we set about arranging transport for Gilded Gamble. She was to travel by trailer up to Dublin and across by boat to Liverpool. We were to collect her from a lairage at Malpas.

Business being over for the moment we thanked our hosts, and the Leonard family, with their impressive yard and house, the kitchen table supporting a magnificent statue of Bula, their most famous son. With me still wearing the slouch hat that seemed as good as any passport, we headed west for the blue Hills of Kerry and the wild Atlantic.

Kerry is arguably the most beautiful of all the Irish counties, with its tall headlands framing the restless green waves, where the heaving swell lies panting and gently growling its disappointment after a 3000-mile journey to the cold rocks of western Ireland; or when the ocean is quiet with the sun sinking in a reddish-golden haze to the west, its rays reflected as a path like a fairy highway heading for the New World, a highway that so many of Ireland's sons and daughters have followed towards an uncertain future.

We stopped the car occasionally to admire the neatly thatched farm cottages, and those of the fishermen, most of them old buildings with walls built of small grey flagstones and mortar with whitewashed borders around the doors and windows, and the thatch held down by netted ropes secured with wooden pegs driven into the walls just below the eaves. Most were single-storey houses nestling in nooks against the hillsides, with their backsides to the prevailing weather. There seemed to be no order in the building. Houses were scattered like chaff in the wind, bearing little relationship to the bohereens that meander through the villages, built in the days when the Irish were Irish and the English were English, before the all-pervading influence of the European Common Market and its cash that has speckled the Irish countryside with ugly Spanish-type bungalows and torn the heart and traditions out of both our islands. Although the Irish seem to be more tenacious to their traditions than us, we seem to be a subservient nation when it comes to buckling down and accepting legislation foisted upon us by foreigners. Strange it is to look back just a few generations and run our fingers over the globe to trace the vastness of the British Empire. I seem to remember being promised a level playing field, free trade and an absolute veto on European legislation. Whatever happened? The loss of our legislative independence as a nation must label old Edward Heath as the Quisling of England.

But enough of politics. Who am I to complain? I would never have made a politician. Quite frankly, I don't like being told what to do and I am sure I would never have been any good at telling other people what to do. On one side of the political divide it always seems to me to be impossible to control the greed of unbridled free enterprise without stifling its flair and initiative. Conversely, the socialist ideal that would employ two men and put them to work side-by-side, then take half the reward from the industrious man and give it to the idle man obviously runs a severe risk of ending up employing two idle men. (Socialism is a noble principle that takes no account of human nature. All men might be born equal but they sure as hell don't end up that way!)

Of course opinions are personal things and perhaps should remain personal; we all look at life from different sides of the fence. For this generation it is very popular to emphasise the adverse and malign effect that mankind has on nature and the natural world. But speaking from the rustic side of the high moorland fence, I have personally been fighting a neverending battle with nature, from the natural flora, as in stinging nettles, brambles, bracken, docks; I probably could go on for at least a paragraph, even bringing in diseases like tuberculosis, brucellosis, blue tongue, scrapie. And as to driving rain, stinging sleet, drifting snow, knee-deep mud and the rest...! Well you see what I mean.

To keep a farm tidy, and running smoothly and efficiently against the predations of the natural world and the politicians, is and always will be a full-time job. One only has to look at the brown-field sites in the inner cities to realise that if our species self destructed – as is entirely possible – it would probably only be fifty or a hundred years before those cheeky innocent little shoots of grass and weed that peep so sweetly up between the concrete and flagstones will have completely reclaimed their world. Of course for the greater part of the population who live on the other side of the fence, and know nothing but tarmac and concrete, the view is entirely different.

Home at last. Gilded Gamble reversed out of the horsebox with a healthy clatter and stood blinking in the sunlight while she surveyed an agricultural scene, competing in rural peace and tranquillity with the one she had so recently left.

Yar Tor seen from the bridlepath between Laughter Hole Farm and Babeny

LIFE MOVES ON

'The old folks used to say that if you saw a raven croak on its back it was always a sure sign of bad luck, and just at that moment I sure as hell believed them…'

HUNTING ADVENTURES

What more could a man want? The whole of Dartmoor and Exmoor to hunt over on a grand Irish chestnut mare that could jump a five-barred gate from a trot. Over the next two seasons, Sarah and I hunted as regularly as farming would allow, our enjoyment only marred by Sarah's bouts of clinical depression, emphasised by two attempts to retire from the struggle of life and avoid the black hole that she saw as the future.

I think perhaps that for someone who has never experienced real depression, it is almost impossible to understand the black depths of despair that infect the mind of the sufferer, even when everything is going well. Both the present and the future apparently seem bleak and desolate.

We tried every avenue of professional help, even going as far as Sarah checking herself temporarily into an institution. I remember the day I drove her and her one little suitcase to the place, as if it was yesterday. One glance at the common room and its 'guests', sitting around the edge of the room with their backs to the wall, some rocking quietly forward and back, others in complete silence, it seemed like a house of the living dead. We both burst into tears and hugged each other. There was absolutely no way I could leave her there. We both felt the atmosphere and the company could only make her worse. Perhaps with hindsight that was a decision that we would both regret. Certainly it was a decision that I have pondered many times over the years.

We were at that time running a small livery business and hacking yard. We also started hiring out some horses for hunting. A good percentage of our customers were the real 'Sloane Square brigade'. At that time the Square Mile was busy and humming with vitality and money. Ferraris, expense accounts and long weekends hunting on Dartmoor were the fashion. Some of our more extraordinary customers provided the local peasantry with a great deal of merriment.

One eccentric couple I remember particularly. The lady used to fly from Frankfurt to London and the gentleman from Texas to London, and after what I guess was presumably a steamy night they motored down together to hunt with us, reversing the exhausting process on the Monday. It was rumoured that the gentleman from Texas was the partner of yet another 'gentleman' who was allegedly caught sucking the toes of a princess. We were on one occasion invited up to town to enjoy the excesses of the Ritz and the Oriental Club. I was never quite sure if we were being displayed as curios or not. Either way it was not a society that either of us felt particularly comfortable with.

One particular young 'Henry' (as in Hooray) arrived to hunt with us early one Saturday morning beautifully attired in hunting pink, top-of-the-range breeches, top hat, mahogany top boots and the rest. He looked and smelled rather beautiful and he had everything apart from the powdered wig. Beau Brummell in his heyday could not have held a candle to the young man. Unfortunately I made the error of assuming that his ability was up to his dress.

We boxed the horses up to the meet which was in a long valley on the other side of Widecombe-in-the-Moor. On being presented with a smart 17-hand gelding that could go a bit, 'his lordship' quietly drew me aside and inquired: 'When I am mounted, should I hold the reins in one hand or both?'! I extracted another £50 from him (very quietly) and supplied a stable girl to put him on a leading rein and trot up and down the valley road with him watching hounds. At the end of the day, 'Sporty Brummell' was entirely satisfied, not at all embarrassed and went back to the city to regale his friends with his hunting adventures among the wild tors of Dartmoor. It transpired that he had never hunted, or even ridden, but was trying to impress his father, an ex-hunting man who had lent him his attire.

I suppose the term 'adventure' typifies that part of hunting that makes it interesting: the unexpected. In that period of my life I had many hunting adventures, including a few nasty falls and a couple of good duckings. One of those was a near drowning in my old friend Mother Dart. It was a dull day in January and it had been raining heavily for about a week. The old girl was in full spate and we were hunting our own ground at Babeny. Consequently I was expected to show the small field of about twenty the best place to cross. We had little choice, as two or three couple of hounds had struggled across and were running hard towards Dunnabridge. I took the crossing at Laughter ford; it was almost an action replay of Father and the rabbits, and in the same spot. I was riding Gilded Gamble as usual and she faced the river without flinching, as she faced everything in life. Now, on a well-schooled horse that doesn't panic, it should be possible to put your leg on and persuade the horse to do a half pass into the river, keeping its head to the current and thus presenting less resistance to the water. Unfortunately, Gamble was at that stage not well schooled, and a bit of tidy dressage was not uppermost in her mind. Eager to cross to the other side and follow hounds she turned broadside to the flood. Now as a rule of thumb, providing the flood does not reach the horse's belly you are usually fairly safe, but once the horse is crossways to the current and the water reaches the belly line with its damming effect you will very soon be up-ended, and up-ended we were in fine style. I collected a sharp blow in the ear from a flailing hoof and remember nothing

Laughter ford in more tranquil conditions

until I found myself grimly gripping a stem of green broom growing out of the far bank, with the tremendous weight of water trying to fill my lungs and tear me back into the main current.

But just like Father some thirty years before, I struggled out onto higher ground, warming myself with the same filthy language, as I guess one does when badly frightened. But once again, luck was with me: the mare scrambled out on my side. The master, Dennis Ferrens, fished half a bottle of Scotch whisky out of his inside pocket and, taking a short run, flung it over the flooded river to land in the moss at my feet. I promptly 'up-ended' it; I don't think it touched the sides. Feeling braver by the minute, I remounted the mare and followed two-and-a-half couple of hounds on a glorious five-mile point, leaving the rest of the unfortunate field on the wrong side of the river.

Some time later we were graced with the extraordinary presence of a real lord, bona fide, brave and completely barmy! It happened that I was sitting in my chair one winter evening toasting my toes in front of quite a decent log fire, when the phone rang. On answering it, I was presented with a slurring but well-educated voice

116

demanding to know if I could supply it with a hunter on the following weekend. I was rather tired and had had 'a drop taken' so I didn't log all the necessary details quite as assiduously as I should have done, merely asking the name and receiving the reply Lord -----. The vaguely squiffy-sounding voice promptly rang off and I was left sitting in front of the fire contemplating the bottom of the glass.

By the next weekend I had thoroughly convinced myself that the call had been a prank by one of my mates but just in case, and being a belt-and-braces sort of chap, I asked the girls to get a hunter ready. The meet was at the Plume of Feathers at Princetown. There was only the possibility of the one customer that day and I was debating whether to start up the lorry or not, thinking that it would be a waste of time, when into the yard struggled an eccentric-looking fellow in a Russian hat. Apparently he was Lord Yarmouth. He appeared to behaving some difficulty in walking; he seemed to be throwing his legs out in front of him, the power apparently coming only from the hips.

Taking one long look at him, I whispered to the girls to tack up two more horses so that we could escort him, thinking that after the level ground and big skies of Norfolk, the boggy and peaty terrain of high Dartmoor with the Dartmoor hounds – even if he had enough strength in his legs and the riding ability – it would be bloody dangerous if not impossible. Much to my relief he asked if he could change out of his casual clothes and Russian hat, producing a full set of very pukka hunting gear. Fortunately there was a high mounting block at the meet, as he was on a grand big 17-hand Shire-cross-hunter called Sefton. The unfortunate part was that Sefton had a hogged mane, which left the poor guy with nothing to hang on to; and as he seemed to have no grip in his legs, apparently only relying on balance like an old rook up an ash tree, we buckled a good stout stirrup leather around Sefton's neck. This was locally known as a JC strap: to avoid blasphemy I will leave the translation to the reader.

The day was a typical Dartmoor day of lowering cloud with a stiff breeze and a spit of rain in the air. When hounds drew away from the meet we paid very careful attention to our illustrious customer, one fore and one aft, still not quite knowing if he was the genuine article. Our concern was utterly groundless. Hounds had been gently working through a newly planted covert of young conifers on the Beardown side of Princetown, when out went a young vixen who had obviously left her knickers somewhere in the vicinity of Burrator reservoir. With a warm day and damp conditions, she left a strong straight scent. Hounds lapped it up and went hell for leather.

Knowing his job, Sefton took off after them like a scalded cat and although our man had his legs rammed out straight, and could only rely on balance, he was hanging on to the JC strap with every appearance of thorough enjoyment. The old horse, for once relishing the lack of interference, stuck his chin out and laying his ears flat went for it, also showing every appearance of enjoyment. Thinking in my naïveté that we were all on the verge of disaster, I rattled my mare on at a sharpish pace in order either to catch up with him or possibly to pick up the pieces, only to see Sefton's backside disappearing over a stiffish stone wall in full and cheerful company. We probably covered twenty to twenty-five miles that day enjoying steady hunting over rough country, and not once did I see Lordy or Sefton turn away from anything that came up in front of them.

At that time of the year, days are short and the dull day had started to offer a stiff drizzle. The light was fading fast when we finished up on the other side of Childe's Tomb and Fox Tor mire. There were only five riders left as we started to hack back in the dark. It was a good long hack over some heavy bogs, also involving a painstaking search for a suitable crossing of the Devonport leat, and eventually we were mightily relieved to see the lights of Princetown ahead. But just in case mistress fate had not dealt us a large enough hand of anxiety, only four of us rode into the light.

> *We cast loose our buff coats,*
> *Each holster let fall,*
> *Shook off both our jackboots...*
> From 'How they brought good news from Ghent to Aix'
> Robert Browning (1812–89)

But unlike 'Dirck, Joris and Co', we hung on to our belts and looked about as for our missing lord, and missing he certainly was. On reflection we had not heard his voice for possibly the last three miles. His very attractive friend was waiting for him and making mild enquiries as to his whereabouts. At this point panic did not exactly set in but it was hovering at close quarters. Our man could not walk easily on dry ground. If he had been dumped in a bog, he most certainly would not have been able to walk back. He would also have had great difficulty crossing the leat. Quite honestly, there was not much to be done, apart from bathing my ulcer in a large whisky and trying to pretend that everything was reasonably in order.

The old wives' tale that a horse will always find its way home is unfortunately a fallacy. If Sefton had been detached from his rider and wandered off, assuming he avoided the bogs he would probably have kept going in any direction until he cleared the moor and found a convenient field gate or some company. It was now as dark as the inside of a cow, the drizzle had turned itself into a thick fog, my ulcer was hurting hellishly, the minute hand of the clock over the bar had described two full circles and we were thinking of informing the police and the local rescue group. (Not that they would have been much good, as according to the indigenous local Dartmoor peasantry, 'they would have been hard pushed to find their own backsides with both hands and a candle'!)

The road outside was certainly not 'a ribbon of moonlight over the purple moor' (from 'The Highwayman' by Alfred Noyes), in fact you could not see across it (the road that is). I was on the point of ringing home to check my public liability insurance and compose a suicide note, when very faintly on the rocky path down from the high moor came the clip clop, clip thump, of a horse with a missing shoe. The relief was amazing. I could have kissed everyone in the pub (and some of them were damned ugly, or covered in mud, or both).

Lord -----, whose incapacity was apparently caused by turning a quad bike over on top of himself on his estate, breezed in as perky as a Jack Russell with two tails, clapped me on the back and ventured the hope that 'no one had been too worried'.

South Devon Hunt meet at the Tavistock Inn, Poundsgate, late 1980s: Jez on Gilded Gamble

After all he had apparently 'once made it across the Texas panhandle', so what was a little slice of Dartmoor?

The day ended pleasantly enough. He and his friend invited us to dinner, we tossed a coin to see who would pay (actually I tossed and he lost). I felt a great deal better after that.

But even with fun, hard work and fresh air, as so often happens in life the merry ripple on the surface often disguises depression and the deep heavy currents below. At the third time of asking the black hole of unremitting anger and despair finally engulfed Sarah's mind and she waved goodbye to the world that so many of us find fascinating, beautiful and interesting.

POACHING

Everyone has their own particular and private way of dealing with loss: mine was darkness and alcohol. I walked many hundreds of miles, travelling through the Dartmoor nights rabbiting, deer hunting and poaching. My best and only friends seeming to be the dog, darkness and alcohol. I drank heavily, not to the extent of becoming alcoholic but certainly far more than was good for me or my relationships with other people. The darkness acted like a bandage. I was free to travel where the fancy took me and fill my freezers with venison, salmon and rabbits, without having to face casual conversation, prying eyes and the time-wasting small talk that goes along with an excess of company. The art of social intercourse was leaving me, but I had a good dog and a good gun, and I gradually gained a deeper knowledge of Dartmoor and its nocturnal wildlife. My night walking, lamping and occasional poaching produced many interesting and amusing incidents.

There was always an abundance of deer, rabbits, fish, hares and the like. The hare has always held a special place in my heart. It has been venerated across the length and breadth of Europe for hundreds or even thousands of years. The old circular drawing of three sitting hares with their ears touching has popped up throughout European history and has even been depicted locally as three rabbits in the same position, 'the tinners' rabbits'.

My love affair with the hare started many years ago when I was mowing an old hay meadow up in the top fields of Oldsbrim beside the Ponsworthy road. I had stopped the tractor in the middle of three acres to answer the call of nature when I noticed something moving in the grass behind the tractor wheel. Thinking it to be the usual mouse or shrew, or some other injured 'timorous beastie', I turned back the freshly cut grass ready to put it out of its misery and there, sitting bolt upright in its tiny form, was a wee scrap of a leveret. As I picked her up to take her to a place of safety in the hedge bank, she sat up in the palm of my hand and tried to box me. That amazing act of bravery and self-preservation from one so small and helpless will remain with me for the rest of my life.

I often wonder why countrymen, farmers, poachers and so on always think of and depict the hare in the female gender? Unless you are talking about a buck hare, the hare is always 'she'. Perhaps it is because hares are wonderful mothers, or perhaps throughout history the hare has breached the gap between the 'hollow' meat of the rabbit or vermin, and the game of the landlord, squire or noble.

One of the best dogs I had in those days was a brindle lurcher called Fly. As with horses, there are only one or two dogs in your life that stand head and shoulders above the others. She and I travelled so many miles together that we always seemed to know what each other was thinking. I don't believe I ever had a dog to equal her in sagacity or cunning. She was born restless and would sleep by the fire with one eye open until I went to the shed to collect the freshly charged battery. And if while donning my boots and overcoat and hat I was stupid enough to tell her where we were going, she would often disappear and I would find her waiting for me at the prearranged spot, even though it were miles from home. At the end of a long night, if I mentioned that we had finished, she would take a rabbit or a hare from me and take it home. She would always be lying on the mat with her share of the uneaten burden between her front legs.

Probably her only annoying habit was that of never catching the same quarry twice. She would always retrieve gently and silently to hand but if the night was wet and windy, and the rabbit or hare slipped from my grasp and bolted off across the field, no amount of encouragement or blasphemy would ever persuade her to chase it again. She would look up at me with her big yellow eyes as if to say, 'You silly bugger, I caught it and you let it go. I'm not catching it twice.'

Another of her little foibles was her intense suspicion of black rabbits. She would run up the beam of the light as usual, but after the first turn of the rabbit she would run with it for a few yards sniffing it, but under no circumstances would she deign to lay a tooth on it. Nowadays her decision would probably not be PC, but that was definitely her opinion of black rabbits and that was that. Like most lurchers she was an inveterate thief but a superb hunting dog, and I loved her dearly.

Probably there is no better way of feeling supremely alive than walking soft-footed upwind over short-cropped Dartmoor grass with a rifle on your back or a good dog by your side. The wind in your face is energising, the darkness all enveloping – and of course there is a freezer to fill. I suppose there is always that tiny piece of latent hunting instinct left in most of us, along with the instinct, or even necessity, of feeding the family. Certainly the quietest and most efficient way of killing rabbits is always a spotlight and a good dog that will retrieve to hand, but when it comes to venison, then the rifle is king.

Dartmoor has its fair share of deer, although in my youth a deer would have been a very rare sight and would have excited comment. Nowadays they have had a population explosion, particularly the beautiful little roe deer which are very common in our area. The nearest population of red deer is probably at Haldon, this side of Exeter, with an occasional big stag straying down from Exmoor, probably after being hard-hunted. The fallow, with their palmated antlers and spots, seem to frequent the wooded areas around the Hennock reservoirs and a few other choice spots that they keep to themselves. The adult roe is only the size of a greyhound, but always looks much bigger in the light and its venison is probably the best eating. If it is marinated and then stewed or casseroled the meat has quite a strong flavour, possibly too strong for the average English palate, but the smell of a nice haunch slowly roasted in a nest of parsnips and baked potatoes emerging from the dark recesses of the Rayburn oven (providing the potatoes have been separately crisped in hot fat) takes a lot of beating, and I bet would even make a hungry vegetarian's teeth water!

Even as a child I always felt thoroughly at home in the dark – providing that is, I was out of doors. I was never quite as comfortable inside a dark house. Only a few times have I been thoroughly alarmed when out at night as an adult. I remember one time when the old dog and I were hunting the high moor. It was a very dark night with a slight breeze, really ideal for the work, and as we were crossing a level area below a large stretch of mire Fly suddenly stopped, and with ears cocked and hackles up she flatly refused to move. She wasn't usually wrong, and obviously her hearing was far more acute than mine. I stopped with her and we both waited, straining our ears and eyes into the darkness. After a few seconds it came again, a low growling and snarling emanating from a clump of rushes, and it seemed to be only about fifteen to twenty yards ahead of us. Fly immediately dropped behind me with some comment about 'you being the bloody alpha male, sort it!'

We probably stood for three or four minutes listening to the blood-chilling noise as it rose and fell on the night air. I did not feel like the alpha male and my hair stood on end, but as Fly had not deserted me and run home, I felt I should respond to her bravery and try to summon up a little of my own. Keeping the spotlight on and the gun cocked, I slowly advanced on the threatening clump of vegetation. Was it vibrating or was that just the breeze? Fly, having made her position quite clear, sat and awaited the outcome. I think my eyeballs were probably travelling half a metre in advance of my nose.

When I eventually got there it turned out to be just a moorland spring disappearing down a hole in a peat hag hidden by sphagnum moss and rushes, cheerfully gurgling as it went! Quite a friendly sound really. Fly was still not completely convinced, and when I called her up to look she merely gave me a glance that would normally accompany the comment, 'Idiot, I told you so, and of course I knew exactly what it was all the time.'

Of course poaching was not always the romantic pastime that it was cracked up to be. It was usually very hard graft through the long nights and frequently with no result, apart from the occasional 'Saltash-rig'! This was an expression that my grandfather frequently used, and which apparently meant a wet backside and no fish. I must admit in my own defence that I was never really a poacher of fish, as my father had taught me to fly fish at an early age and it was a sport that I enjoyed, and have taken great pleasure in ever since. In those early days there were a few expert salmon and sea trout poachers, and of course there were many more salmon and sea trout in the rivers in the middle of the last century.

One of the favourite poachers' methods in those days was to prepare a home-made bomb from an old whisky bottle half full of wet sand with a clip top. A couple of nodules of carbide were poked down the neck of the bottle and the top clipped back on. The bottle was then placed gently on the surface of the pool and released to weave its silent way down among the inhabitants. Carbide is a chemical that turns to gas when wet (it was used for lighting on carriages and in bicycle lamps as a flammable gas before electricity). Of course with the wet sand and the sealed bottle it only took a few minutes to produce a large enough explosion to stun most of the fish in the pool. The rest was easy, providing you got away quickly in case the bailiff had heard the bang.

In more modern times I remember a respectable middle-aged middle-class gent who moved into the local village and spent several summers removing many of the best salmon and sea trout around the local waters. It was well known locally that he took a great many fish, but no one could ever catch him at it. He regularly walked all the local rivers with his Labrador dog and a long thumbstick and, apart from his long overcoat and Polaroid glasses, he was the picture of well-exercised respectability. I can't remember exactly how he was eventually caught, but suffice to say the thumbstick was the answer. He had ingeniously hollowed it out and passed a wire down through its centre with a noose on the end. The rest I can leave to your imagination. Greed was his downfall, like most poachers who are caught. I suppose that if you have to do something wrong, then it is best not to make a habit of it.

Having stated from personal experience that poaching is not always a romantic pastime, it is certainly not always a profitable pastime either. I well remember a mate of mine who was a member of one of the local gypsy families and an experienced poacher. He returned from a couple of days in Northern Ireland with a big brindle lurcher-type dog. It stood thirty inches at the shoulder, was very broad in chest and muzzle and wore an expression not unlike a bag of chisels.

Two of the lads took him on his first outing. I suppose they were keen to see his credentials in case they needed to demand their money back. The venue for the evening was Haldon Forest near Exeter, running beside the A38 dual carriageway. As previously noted, that area of woodland accommodates many deer. The master criminals drove quietly in with the old van, and sure enough they soon ran into a small family party of deer. Mister Paddy the dog did exactly what it said on his tin and pulled down a young hind in very short order. Unfortunately just as the two subordinates in his pack were closing in on his kill, a blue flashing light accompanied by a siren came speeding down the dual carriageway. Our two worthies, being a trifle shy, immediately threw the carcass and the dog into the van and ran down to the road to see which way the law had gone. It smelled suspiciously like a tip-off when the law turned into the wood at the far end. This turn of events obviously initiated a mad scramble back to the van, only to be greeted by the pack leader having his supper, and between growling mouthfuls of venison showing off a handsome set of dentures. I believe that it took the boys in blue all of two hours to extract dog and venison from the stolen vehicle, by which time the birds had flown and were safely tucked up in bed.

Of course they do say that love is blind, but I believe that the love some men have for a good dog is often blinder. A good dog for night work ought to share many of the characteristics that his master should have, and frequently doesn't. The ideal dog should always be unobtrusive, both in voice and figure; obviously a dog that gives vent to his feelings with a bark or a wine is an abomination and quickly leads to discovery, much the same as the poacher that gives vent to his, after a few pints of 'tongue loosener' at the public house. Many poachers and gamekeepers have ruined a night's work with a slip of the tongue in the wrong company. Alcohol both loosens the tongue and increases the bravado, and there is no easier meat to be had than when you know the opposition is somewhere else.

Many of the older generation of poachers were young men through the great Depression of the 1930s, when poaching was not just sport but was often necessary to feed a hungry family. They were generally hard, quiet and unobtrusive men, mostly good amateurs who didn't make money from the game: they were brought to it by necessity. Many were countrymen born and bred, often working on the land so they had a thorough knowledge of the countryside and its flora and fauna. Frequently walking or bicycling to work, they always had a keen eye for signs of game and normally consumed the evidence. I suppose looking at it through the shafts of a wheelbarrow, neither rabbit nor hare in our area were cultivated by the farmer or the squire.

Of course with poaching, as with any other business, the quieter the waters the deeper they run, and the quiet man that says the least and keeps his own counsel is often the man that does the most; although they do say that Shakespeare, the great bard himself, was a useful deer poacher, but perhaps that was the exception that proved the rule.

Along with being quiet and unobtrusive in every aspect of life, the efficient poacher has also to be physically strong. Carrying half a dozen rabbits home in the small hours is quite a task, but to carry even a small roebuck for a mile or two over rough country is bloody hard work. You can be left with the awkward decision of paunching it on the spot and leaving the evidence, but having a lighter load to carry and a great deal of blood down your back, or carrying it whole, making the load at least one third heavier. Leaving a carcass to be collected at leisure in daylight is not an option, even on your own land. The carcass will probably be partially devoured by foxes, badgers, or other people's dogs, and if poached it is surprising who you might find sitting quietly watching it in the morning.

I well remember one amusing incident when a young sportsmen-cum-gamekeeper in the district, having been given the tip-off by the squire that there was a notorious old poacher in the area who usually frequented the local hostelry, determined to keep a strict eye on the rogue. Consequently, whenever the miscreant was not warming his bits at the pub fire, he was assumed to be poaching. The conscientious young gamekeeper travelled many miles around the country after dark, braving all the elements in his endeavours to catch the man at it. Finally frustrated and dejected he confided in a local farm labourer, only to be met with the comment: 'Oh, didn't you know? Old Jack spends most nights back at your place entertaining your wife!' The young man left the area soon afterwards, not being able to handle the winks and knowing looks. Happily, his wife went with him.

Looking back thirty or forty years there were of course the remnants of the less wholesome sports as in dog and cock fighting. The Old English gamebird was quite common in the area as they were low maintenance and flighty enough to take care of themselves, and usually avoid the foxes. For many years we bred the Old English Willow-legged Ginger, not for fighting but as general farmyard poultry. They were self-sufficient and tough, both mentally and physically. The little blighters would peck their way out of the egg, roll up their sleeves and glare around with a 'Who's next?' expression. They were never happier than when having a good scrap. They were also very good eating, rather gamey and much the size and flavour of a pheasant.

BAD BIRD

It was a bitterly cold day in February when Bad Bird joined us. 'Earth stood hard as iron' and all that, the game hens had been 'stealing nests' in hay racks, lofts, old bunches of stinging nettles, or generally any place that was particularly unsuitable for rearing a family.

Early one morning as I walked across the top yard on my first light rounds, I happened to notice a broken egg that had not been there the previous evening and it was unoccupied. A little further away lay a tiny yellow scrap of bad temper, frozen to the ground. At first I thought it was dead until I heard the bad language. I took my pocket knife and chipped it out of the ice, placed it in my hat and thus transported the sweet little fellow back to the Rayburn oven in the kitchen. There were to be many times in the next couple of years that we all wished he had been left in the oven and properly stuffed! If ever there was a small package that contained a mixture of courageous loyalty, endearing cheek and bad temper with malign intent in equal measures, Bad Bird was it.

After the little sod had warmed up (and just before he started to roast) we placed him gently and delicately on the hearth mat whereupon he promptly attacked the cat. Our next problem was what to feed him on. (With the benefit of hindsight we should have let him starve.) The problem did not trouble us for long as he was obviously destined to be a cannibal. I hard-boiled an egg (which presumably had the potential to be a sibling), draped a towel around my shoulders and there he perched for a week or two as I fed him from time to time with bits of hard-boiled egg on the end of a cocktail stick. He obviously relished the altitude, the seat of authority and the occasional lump of my ear when I didn't come up with the goods within his time frame.

His favourite evening occupation was watching the television from my shoulder and attacking it with vigour if anyone in the picture dared to make eye contact with me or him. After a while friends, family, dogs, cats, horses and anyone one or thing else that valued its life, avoided me like the plague.

There was staying at that time an old friend of ours, a retired rugby-playing black cab driver from London who had witnessed and ignored most of the depravities of the great metropolis. 'John', unknown to us, was in the habit of going for a morning stroll before breakfast. On this particular morning I was making an early cup of tea and gazing sleepily across the yard to the footpath when I spied a thickset bald, middle-aged but obviously extremely active man doing quite a passable hornpipe with gay abandon and much gesticulation and flailing of arms. On hurrying across the yard for a closer and more intimate inspection I discovered Bad Bird had taken him for an intruder and was fastened securely to his shin, pecking away with the rapidity of a hammer drill or possibly a woodpecker from a Tom and Jerry cartoon. After John had bolted from the scene of battle, Bad Bird's victory feathers were soon unruffled. It took at least twenty-four hours, a good meal and a few pints to unruffle John's!

MAD COW DISEASE

It must have been some time in the reign of Bad Bird – probably during his first winter as the undisputed dictator of Babeny – that my dear old Mother Dart did her very best to ruin me. There had for some days been a relentless and vindictive wind bustling depression after depression in from the Atlantic. The high moor and all the blanket bogs had soaked up as much moisture as they could comfortably deal with, and the river was running at its high winter level. At that time the cattle were alternately feeding on kale behind the electric fence at Babeny and then wandering back to the newtake to graze on rough molinia grass and heather on the western side of the river valley. Just as I considered the winter had no more rain to offer, it took us by surprise and started to rain in greater earnest.

Looking across the valley towards Laughter and Bellever tors, the rain sheeted

Laughter Tor, seen from Bellever Tor

down in grey moving curtains for hours on end. The tiny peaty rivulets started to run from the saturated bogs, chuckling maliciously as they joined hands and explored bigger gullies leading to streams and eventually to the river. In its turn the old river started to stir and swell. Odd bits of stick, pine cones and general flotsam began to find their way into the main current from the tributary streams and within an hour-and-a-half Dartmoor's main artery had swollen into a filthy muddy raging torrent, sweeping all before it.

Meanwhile the cattle, which at that stage of the day were sheltering under the newtake wall on the other side of the river, were driven by hunger pangs and the lure of a belly full of turnips and kale to begin to meander back towards the crossing at Blackator rocks. At just about the same time, acting on some sixth sense, I took the dog and hurried down to the river bank on the eastern side of the crossing.

All herds have their leader and theirs was old Mabel (a stupid name for a cow) but she was a fine sensible old matriarch and she led the herd of roughly one hundred head in all shapes and sizes including some calves, most of them true to a breeding line that I had held for many years. At last they came to the water's edge. I was not particularly worried at that stage, even though I was looking at my entire stock and income for years to follow, with of course no insurance against acts of God, and with an unsympathetic bank manager sitting on a healthy overdraft… perhaps I should have been.

Mabel, true to her age and responsibility, pulled up short at the water's edge and stood on the wet slippery bank gazing at the flood with the experience and sure knowledge that it was just not crossable. For a moment all was well, but as she was about to turn back, a flighty young heifer that had been standing directly behind her and was obviously in season suddenly decided to mount the old girl in the ridiculous way that cattle do. Mabel, using the ring craft and experience of a lifetime, twisted and swung away from the torrent but with half a ton of younger cow on her back, the peaty bank gave way and catapulted them both into the water. The older cow, bellowing her anger and fear as the water hit her, struck out for the home bank. The rest of the cattle, blindly following their leader as cattle do, pushed forward and dropped into the flood behind her. The larger heavier cattle could just touch the bottom with their feet and the current promptly rolled them over. One by one they disappeared around the bend of the river, bawling with fear and blowing plumes of spray.

The younger lighter cattle fared better as their feet didn't touch anything solid and they bobbed away on the current making valiant endeavours to swim. (If you have ever seen a film of migrating wildebeest crossing a flooded river in Africa, you can imagine the scene.) They were all vainly endeavouring to come home across the river, towards me, while I charged up and down the bank screaming like a lunatic, feeling thoroughly sick and dizzy as I grabbed sticks, stones and anything to hand to throw at them and try to get them to stay back. Meanwhile the old sheepdog, sensing my fear and anguish and always willing to help, jumped in and promptly disappeared under a struggling, bawling and terrified herd of her charges.

In that one moment everything that I had worked for and aspired to for so many years had disappeared before my eyes. In that spell of intense anguish there was just nothing to be done. I walked up the bank onto higher ground and vomited behind a tree. It was an old oak, and as I looked up through the branches to the sky, a raven passed low overhead and rolled in the air as he croaked. The old folks used to say that if you saw a raven croak on its back it was always a sure sign of bad luck, and just at that moment I sure as hell believed them.

But I suppose life always has its ups and downs, and after a few minutes Tessa the sheepdog came trotting up the bank looking rather wet and apologetic, bless her. She had kept swimming until she found an easy exit from the flood, as dogs usually do. She promptly nuzzled under my coat and licked my hand, suggesting a survey of the damage ought to be in order. Together we travelled the bank for maybe a quarter of a mile, and Lady Luck must have been with us that day. It appeared that most of the cows had struggled out on one bank or the other and were standing in forlorn and shivering bunches, contemplating pneumonia. Just at that moment a shaft of sunlight shone through a blue patch between the clouds, 'sailor's trousers' and all that, and the

The East Dart river just above its confluence with the Wallabrook

blue patches slowly spread into a warm and sunny afternoon. Religion tempted me once more but unfortunately I had been far too busy to pray to anybody. It took two whole days to reassemble the herd, and on inspection the total damage amounted to two calves with respiratory problems and one missing cow.

The missing cow, however, did not have luck on her side. The next day with the river still in full spate I discovered her a mile below the ford, just past the confluence of the Wallabrook and the Dart. The old dear was draped artistically around a large boulder in midstream. She was a macabre sight. The heavy current was moving her legs forward and back as if she were still alive and struggling, while her head rested cosily against the cold stone with one ear protruding above the current, sporting a red eartag with the name Babeny clearly visible.

Looking back over the passage of time, the sequence of my actions from then on were plainly ludicrous, but with hindsight rather amusing. She was in the centre of a flooded river miles from any road or track, and it seemed that the only possibility of post mortem recovery was by helicopter. The first thought that my agitated mind threw up was the strong desire that she should not be recognised as a Babeny cow. This was partly from a fear of prosecution under the pollution laws (visions of her basking on the mudflats opposite Dartmouth Royal Naval College still waving her Babeny eartag sent a chill through my soul); partly from the fear of ridicule by my neighbours who would consider it careless to lose a cow; and partly from the inbred desire of most older countrymen 'not to let anyone else know my bloody business'.

As I could get nowhere near her – and there was nothing sticking up to lasso – I ran back to the farm and collected my 12-bore and a pocket full of cartridges, the theory being that if I could shoot out the eartag it would give me time to think. Had I thought, the sight of an idiot dancing about on a river bank shooting a dead cow should have raised a smile, but from then on the situation went downhill fast.

I had used up my pocket full of cartridges and completely shredded her ear, but it was still managing to hold onto the tag. More desperate measures were obviously called for. Noticing a large willow tree standing proudly on the bank, I suddenly realised that if I could call on the remembered skills of ten years of timber felling I could, by holding one root and spinning the tree, just possibly land the top of it across the carcass and the rock, providing me with a horizontal ladder.

I immediately abandoned the 12-bore and tramped home through the rain for a chainsaw, silently praying that no one would come along the river bank in the meantime. Eventually armed with a stout pair of waders, a chainsaw and two strong ropes, I arrived back and surveyed the tree carefully. Allowing for the angle of tilt and the gusting storm–force wind, I took a neat dip out of the side facing the carcass. Bringing the main cut in opposite at an elevation of about four inches, I carefully left one hawser root to pull the tree round. Much to my delight (and rather to my surprise) it landed inch perfect.

So far luck was still with me, but the interesting bit was yet to come. Leaving the chainsaw a little way up the bank, I took the ends of the two ropes and crawled rather gingerly out across the willow with the surging muddy torrent lapping my knees and straining at the tree. Securely tying the end of each rope to a leg 'fore and aft' I retraced my crawl back to the bank, incidentally filling my waders as I went. (It is generally not a good idea to fall into flooded rivers with waders on as the waders, retaining the air, float to the top leaving your head and breathing apparatus, which generally contains less air, underwater!) When both ropes were in their turn secured to the willow stump, I firmly grasped the chainsaw and made the repeat journey to the carcass, sharing my balance between the rock, the willow and the cow.

I rammed my hat down on my head in an effort to keep the driving rain from sluicing into my eyes; I then slowly stood upright and started the chainsaw. Now it is at times like these one tends to suffer an attack of tunnel mentality, and it is quite easy in the trauma of the moment to lose sight of everything apart from that which is directly under one's nose. It is surprising how a sharp chainsaw will make considerable headway through a carcass! Unfortunately, along with the speed and efficiency comes a heavy spray of blood and guts and bone that engulfs the operator and leaves him looking horrendous enough to put any X-rated nightmare to shame. It was in the middle of this macabre operation that I heard, above the roar of the river, my old dog bark a sharp warning. Glancing over my shoulder to the nearer bank, and only six or seven yards distant, I found myself looking directly into the horror-struck faces of two perambulating ladies and a poodle with a pink collar. All three were well dressed for the occasion, but that in no way inhibited the stark terror in their eyes.

The older lady, taking a sharp step backwards, sat down in a puddle. Her younger companion, after helping her to her feet, risked one horror-struck look over her shoulder as all three scuttled off downstream towards Dartmeet as if the devil and all his henchmen were close on their heels. Feeling that if I chased after them with some sort of explanation they would probably all have died of fright, I continued with the only sensible course of action and severed the cow down the middle, so freeing both halves to float away from the rock, while still attached to the stump of the willow.

So far so good. I was now on a roll. My next problem was how to extract the two halves from the river and transport them to a place of safety, cremation or burial, or at least get them away from the uneducated and prying eyes of the general public, the Water Board, DEFRA and so on. This was not easy as it was obviously impossible to get a wheeled or tracked vehicle anywhere near the scene of action. Options were severely limited. Digging was impossible as the area was solid granite. Roast beef was obviously also impossible according to the weather and, had either option been available, dragging half a ton of wet beef out of a flooded river would be difficult in itself. My mind had momentarily drawn a blank and I was sorely tempted to run a knife across the ropes and consign a hearty meal to the Dartmouth crab population.

But, as before, the mind works at high-speed overdrive in desperate situations and in a blinding flash of light my salvation appeared before me. Why had I not thought of him before? Humphrey was my salvation and the only guy willing and strong enough for the task, especially as I paid his wages (mostly in oats and horse nuts)! Humphrey was a grand old horse fully 17 hands high, half Shire half Thoroughbred, but very much favouring the Shire. In the old days he would have been a farm draught horse, very much like Blackie and Pleasant. With his heavily feathered feet and a kind and willing disposition, nothing ever worried Humphrey. He was absolutely bombproof.

My idea was to take a heavy cotton rope and make an improvised collar around his neck, and with two running lines back to the rope that secured half the cow, it should be simple to extract and remove the two problems without the aid of heavy machinery. Humphrey, sensing something mildly out of the ordinary, allowed himself to be led out of the yard and down to the river. I backed him up and attached the lines to the rope that tethered the front end of the cow, which was hard against the bank and under water. I led the old boy forward and to my joy, he leaned heavily into the collar and started to pull as if he had been at it all his life. The strain on the rope was considerable and after a few struggling yards, he ill-advisedly turned his head and glanced over his shoulder.

Now Humphrey had never pretended to be as brave as Theseus, and the sight of something akin to a Minator, horns and all, emerging bloody and dripping from the raging torrent immediately behind him, suddenly (and to my mind inexplicably) turned the old gent into a wild-eyed snorting Thoroughbred. With one gigantic bound and a sideways kick at me, he brought his ghoulish load up onto the bank where it promptly took a gigantic bound after him. This was more than his nerves could stand and he was last seen galloping at a high rate of knots through the gorse and heather with his tail on end like a startled ferret, trailing broken ropes and heading for the sanctuary of his stable.

THE OTHER SIDE OF LIFE

It must have been somewhere about the same time as the near disaster of the flood, when coming into tea one Saturday afternoon (after spending the morning delivering a couple of loads of firewood which I was selling at the time to augment the small farm income) I was greeted by my new wife, Linda, who informed me that we ought to go to Newton Abbot on the Monday and visit the Oxfam shop or somewhere similar, as I didn't have a lounge suit and we couldn't afford to buy a new one. Apparently I had been summoned.

You will understand I hope, Dear Reader, that I do not mean summoned in the legal sense. Suffice it to say that in a few days' time I was to find myself walking up the steps of St Paul's Cathedral in the close and esteemed company of one or two slightly more famous names of the time, as in Margaret Thatcher, James Callaghan and like. It was of course 29 July 1981 and the wedding of the decade. My concern of the moment (among others) was not if my £3.50 suit would past muster, but rather more that if any fanatical marksman from over the water should try a pot-shot at the politicians, he would be polite enough to leave me standing. I probably need not have worried: we had just been treated to the sight of comedian Spike Milligan capering around in front of St Paul's making a Goon of himself, and it occurred that if anyone deserved to be shot it probably wasn't me.

We sat as a congregation of 3500 waiting for the great entrance. For a very few moments you could have heard a pin drop. Apart from us there were allegedly 750 million viewers watching the occasion throughout the world.

Eventually from somewhere deep in the city we heard the distant roar of 600,000 larynxes slowly pulsating towards us, until at length Prince Charles arrived to claim his undeniably beautiful twenty-year-old bride, Lady Diana Spencer, from his rather portly father-in-law-to-be, Earl Spencer. The Archbishop of Canterbury officiated at the ceremony. Both Charles and Diana slightly fluffed their lines (Charles bequeathing his possessions but forgetting worldly), probably quite a good idea with the advantage of hindsight; and Diana getting her fiancé's Christian names the wrong way around.

Perhaps the most beautiful part of the ceremony was when Dame Kiri Te Kanawa filled St Paul's with a voice so beautiful and pure that it made the hair stand up on the back of my neck and a shiver run down my spine. I had never in my naïveté realised that a human voice could sound so perfect – it being quite probable that up to that time I had never heard a live voice raised for any reason other than to the berate an idle sheepdog or curse a cow.

The great metropolis did not hold us long. Those of us who had braved the journey scuttled back to the safety of Dartmoor as swiftly as possible. I learned a few things that day. Among the major points were the undeniable fact that everything cost twice as much as it did at home, people did not relish being spoken to and it was probably not a good idea to look them straight in the eye. I have only ventured as far as our capital city once since that occasion. Nowadays I seem to get homesick if I travel past Exeter, and I am only in my comfort zone when I can see the hills and tors of Dartmoor.

The next occasion, and hopefully the last, was a garden party at Buckingham Palace where I found myself probably one of the very few people in the country not particularly impressed with the Princess of Wales, although I found the contrast between her height and the diminutive stature of Her Majesty the Queen rather a surprise (something that you would not notice on the television). I might be an old cynic, but in general I have the utmost respect for the Royal Family. Theirs is not an easy job, certainly not a job I would like to have thrust upon me from birth. The Queen might be the steward of a great deal of money but after all, the old dear doesn't bury it in the garden: it comes around again to a great many people, and businesses and charities. Personally I would far prefer a fine winter's day on the common with a ferret and nets to a royal garden party – although perhaps that's not quite the whole truth. As I sit at my desk I have hanging on the wall opposite me a small picture of which I am quite proud. It is a photograph of Charles, Diana and the boys at Harry's christening: 'To Mister Wilkinson with all good wishes for Christmas and the New Year, signed Charles and Diana.'

RABBITING

But time it goes on and while the republicans were muttering in their beer, quite a selection of the 'young and upwardly mobile' were hunting in the West Country, some of them with us. At that time I was on the committee of the South Devon Hunt and I remember Mr Hewitt, among others, hunted with us quite regularly.

Of course rabbiting with a ferret and nets was and is the preferred leisure activity of many of the farm workers. My father, grandfather and uncle, usually accompanied by Peter Hannaford, traditionally set aside Boxing Day for rabbiting. This was long before the more modern tradition of rearing pheasants for the sport of shooting arrived in our area. I say 'sport' with a certain amount of caution as I am quite fond of birds of most species – apart from perhaps the corvines – and I am particularly fond of farmyard poultry, so I run the risk of making myself unpopular with the local middle classes, including perhaps some of my immediate family, by putting forward my mild reservations. It always seems to me that to rear a pheasant poult and feed it by hand to the point when it looks on you as its friend and benefactor and follows you around like a chicken, and then to encourage it to fly, only to endeavour to blow it out of the air in a cloud of blood and feathers, is a little harsh.

I have on occasion joined shooting parties but to date I have never actually shot a pheasant. Not I might add through any fellow feeling or a really strong moral objection, but as my brain tumour left me with tunnel vision I am only able to see the target for the split second that it is directly in front of me, so the pheasants and my slight moral principles make good and easy bedfellows. Most other field sports sit comfortably with me. The fox is and always has been my arch enemy, 'the cunning thief of the night'. He knows exactly where he stands and he knows that we are enemies from birth and acts accordingly. Equally my two favourite quarries, the rabbit and the sea trout, are pursued with both predator and prey possessing the full knowledge of the rules. The sea trout season runs from the early spring to the end of September when the fish have finished spawning. Rabbiting, on the other hand, is normally practised in the winter when there aren't any 'milky does' (females heavy in young) or baby bunnies. So back to ferret and nets.

Being primarily a winter sport and often involving waiting around in the cold, I always made sure I had a good tweed coat and sound boots with no holes or leaks in them. The rabbit, or *Oryclolagus cuniculus* as I was instructed to call it by my Latin master at school (and a fat lot of use that was), has been woven into the psyche of the countryman for a few hundred years. I remember when I was very young, before that flea-borne disease myxomatosis decimated the rabbit population in 1954, most of Grandfather's fields at Babeny had a bare strip of grass or crops around each of them extending some two or three yards from the hedgerow. With small Dartmoor fields, this could add up to the destruction of one-sixth or one-fifth of the crop. It was not unusual to look up the hedge of a two- or three-acre field and see thirty or forty rabbits; and although Dartmoor never lent itself to arable crops if anyone was brave enough to try and grow a field of oats, when the binder had cut nearly to the middle of the field, the last half acre or so would literally be moving with rabbits that had spent the summer in the oats and were completely disoriented.

As kids we had a great time with the dogs trying to catch them. It was not that hard, as many of the silly things had not been back to the hedgerow for most of their life and being deprived of cover would run around and try to hide under the sheaves of corn, not being quite sure which way was home. Although the Latin name sounds Roman, as I suppose it should, this mixed blessing was not necessarily their fault. Apparently the rabbit was introduced to this country by the Normans. The Bayeux Tapestry shows them carrying baskets full of rabbits, presumably for an introductory breeding programme. One of my strongest memories as a child was the overwhelming stink of rotten meat after the myxomatosis had arrived and every little gorse bush or hedge had its cloud of flies and overwhelming smell of death. It was a cruel disease and involved much suffering.

Back in the days when Dartmoor was an industrial area the rabbit was a major food source for tin miners and agricultural workers alike. Many history books show the old circle with the three tinners' rabbits inside with the points of their ears touching. Count the rabbits and then count the ears? A clever symbol indicating the importance of the rabbit. After all, post the collapse of the mining industry the rabbit helped feed us through two world wars and the great depression of the 1930s. So important was it that there were many warrens built across Dartmoor to conserve and farm the rabbit. Two of the better-known examples are near the Warren House Inn on the Princetown to Moretonhampstead road and Warren Pitts on the side of Vag Hill, opposite Dartmeet. These warrens were man-made, usually piles of loose stone roughly covered with earth or turf, often with a vermin trap consisting of low walls running in a V-shape leading small predators into a drop-down slate trap.

Personally I always preferred to work a ferret on what we called ground buries, which were natural warrens made by the rabbits themselves, often in open country with the rabbits grazing a substantial area around the warren and keeping the grass very short. Consequently I found the holes easier to net, and it was much easier to see and dispatch the captive quickly. The tight grazing of the rabbits has for many generations helped the biodiversity of Dartmoor by keeping down the young leaves and shoots of scrub gorse and brambles, and encouraging smaller plant life like trefoil, vetches, violets. The grazing of agricultural livestock has done the same.

Even Charles Darwin and his colleagues so many years ago noticed this, but it appears to be beyond the comprehension of the sadly misguided so-called experts from DEFRA. It is a curious fact that we, as farmers, have husbanded Dartmoor for probably 5000 years or more, and on the admission of DEFRA we have created a landscape and a biodiversity that is second to none in the West of England. But we are now plagued with hordes of bureaucrats (most of whom have probably never done a hard day's work in their life and certainly never actually produced anything) rewarding themselves with large salaries and long holidays while endeavouring to inform us how to take care of an environment that we in fact created. It's a strange world. I suppose parasitic is too hard a word for people who presume themselves to be gainfully employed, but it has always been a fact of life that some people will take an easy ride on the backs of others. I apologise again, dear reader, for straying into the realms of politics. Perhaps there is still a little of my feisty suffragette Grandmother coursing through my veins with the blood that can't quite make its mind up as to its colour.

'THE FRIENDLY CORNISH'

Going back half a generation, the small tenanted hill farm did not render a really adequate living to its occupants. Although we grew a lot of our own vegetables and killed our own meat, times were often a bit tight. So along with the farming and the firewood business, I started contract shearing in the early summer. This was useful additional income for maybe ten or twelve weeks.

We had always kept sheep, and gradually upgraded from hand to motorised shears, powered by a small and smelly Briggs and Stratton petrol engine. Although I liked shearing and prided myself on being quite quick, the noise and fumes in a hot shearing shed were at first unpleasant. Fortunately we soon moved ahead to quieter electric shears.

This must have been about the same time as the famous shearer Godfrey Bowen came to this country from the colonies (Australia!) on the other side of the world and showed us just what sort of dunces we were at the job. He had a series of shearing demonstrations all over the country. Fortunately one was quite near to us at Tavistock, and several of us muddy-footed local turnip crunchers went down to watch him and hopefully take the mick. I must admit we left with smiles on the other side of our faces. We had mostly been with sheep all our lives and couldn't understand how a man could shear so skilfully at that speed. This fellow was knocking out some three hundred sheep a day, whereas we could probably only manage a hundred on a good day with compliant sheep. The man was a genius and showed us a whole new way of handling the sheep.

We had always been used to sitting a sheep as still as possible on the floor, or sometimes on a table, and moving around and around the animal. As I said before if you were ambidextrous it was a great advantage. This guy sat the sheep upright between his legs and turned the sheep with his legs and feet, putting less strain on the back. And instead of going around the sheep, he basically sheared it up and down, including the longest blow, which followed the backbone from the tail to between the ears.

The easiest sheep to shear were our own Scotch half-breds and they were a gift. They were wild enough to sit in terrified immobility and devoid of wool on the bellies and half the legs. (By half the legs I mean that each leg was only woolly halfway down. Not, as it might appear, only woolly on two legs and naked on the other two!)

In pursuance of my new enterprise I advertised in the 'Situations wanted' column of the local and semi-local press and to my delight got a good selection of replies.

One such was from a Cornish farmer who also owned a magnificent hotel on the north coast. At least it obviously started out as a magnificent hotel but I think the farmer-owner, who was moving on in years, was perhaps trying to ride two horses in the same race. The farm clung tenaciously to the wild Cornish cliffs while the Castle Hotel, which stood as a bulwark against anything the weather could throw at it, scorned any form of shelter and appeared wrapped in a dream world of chronological immobility and decorous neglect.

Having found the place and admired the magnificent views out over the Atlantic I was somewhat at a loss as to whether to use the front door or the tradesman's entrance, or perhaps I should go and look for the farm sheds. A quick glance revealed no sheds, so one half of my schizophrenic nature took me to the front door.

A magnificent peal of the Castle Hotel doorbell announced my arrival and set my nerves jangling, thinking to myself that the establishment was perhaps a cut or two above my usual shearing haunts. The demanding terms of the bell having been closely followed by a long silence, I prepared to retreat to my old truck full of shearing gear which the other half of my character had demanded that I leave around the corner. Before I had taken more than a few steps I was hailed by a large Cornish voice issuing from behind the door. As after a second or two it appeared that no one was prepared to open it, I pulled myself together and entered.

Standing in the spacious hall was a large friendly Cornishman who precisely fitted the voice. His dress was peculiar, the bottom half was breeches and boots (as in farmer), the top half was collar and tie (as in hotelier). My hand was grasped by something resembling a bear's paw and the right hand side of my body was pumped up and down in such a jovial and friendly manner that I felt rather like the bottom labourer in a saw pit.

Had I been older and wiser a little alarm bell would have rung in my brain, triggered by the over-friendly reception and the fact that my advertisement had been answered at a distance of some eighty miles or so. Didn't they have any contract shearers in Cornwall? Answer: yes they did and some bloody good ones too, and mostly a little wiser than me.

Anyway I was escorted to the sheds that had been hiding in a little cove; they were tightly packed with a hundred or so sheep which had obviously just been gathered from the cliffs and the seashore in readiness. Fine, thinks I to myself. I'll be out of here by teatime and home a good bit before dark. ('Stupid boy!')

They were not in bad condition and they were heavily fleeced with wool from their teeth to their toenails, and their close proximity to the sea throughout the year had left their fleeces full of ingrained salt. Now depending on the sheep, a couple of sets of blades would last me most of the day. With those buggers I had to change cutters every two or three sheep. Each sheep took at least twice as long to shear as it should have done. Bought wit being always better than taught wit, as old Peter used to say. Before the end of the day I had run out of sharp cutters and, much to the delight of the locals and the amusement of the farmer-hotelier, had to go back the next day and finish the job.

So much for the friendly Cornish, but I suppose they can play rugby and lift heavy things! Come to think of it even the blasted trees lean back towards Devon, obviously trying to come home.

THE NOBLE SEA TROUT

A life predominantly concerned with agriculture, horses, fencing and timber is normally governed by the hours of daylight, particularly in the summer months when it is possible to put in a standard eighty-hour week. Fortunately I love my work and like to wake up each morning looking forward to the possibility of attaining some small goal or improving something around the farm or business. Without these minor aims and ambitions I suppose life would not have much point or meaning. They give a reason, at least, to roll out in the morning.

But 'all work and no play makes Jack a dull boy', they say! And old Mother Dart came to my rescue once again and let me play with her children. I have already mentioned my high regard for the sea trout and those that go down to the 'water in boots' to catch them. The sea trout is one of the wanderers of the piscean brigade. He is basically an ordinary brown trout that behaves like so many of the more interesting animals, fish – and for that matter people – who become bored with their surroundings and go in search of something better.

Spawned in the gravel beds of the high mountain streams and tributaries of the great moorland rivers – the Dart, the Teign, the Tavy (and a couple that lost their way and headed for the Bristol Channel, the Taw and the Torridge) – one of thousands or even millions of tiny eggs that run the gauntlet of the heavy winter

The East Dart river below Babeny

floods and the predations of their cannibalistic family and other roving predators like elvers, water ouzels and so on, the egg hatches out after a couple of months, depending on the temperature of the water. When hatched, the eggs produce a tiny translucent creature (an alevin) with an umbilical egg sac hanging under his chin. During the alevin stage of up to a month the little fellow enjoys the contents of his yolk sac and when that is exhausted he becomes a fry. At this stage he has to face the big bad world and fend for himself! This aptitude for survival will eventually turn him into one of the most active and hard-fighting fish in the world, and I have always loved him for it.

As a fry the sea trout appears as merely an ordinary brown trout and it feeds on small flies, nymphs, insect larva, crustacea and other aquatic life until it grows into its next stage of life as a parr. It would then be about six inches long and probably anything up to three years old. Now being a sort of fishy teenager or 'hobbledy hoy' he presumably makes his decision to leave the old folks at home, like most teenagers with anything about them, and travel down to the sea.

To facilitate the next part of his adventure he develops salt-secreting cells and assumes a silver coat, much finer and gaudier than the stay-at-home natives. Now being dressed for the part he heads for the saline 'ball' in and around the estuaries, and calls himself a smolt. The sea trout (or peel), unlike the salmon, tends to stay around the coastal water and estuaries. Our young smolt probably represents only 0.5 percent of the eggs originally laid. I said he was a fighter and he obviously came first in a race of many hundreds of thousands, as I suppose we all did. He may return to the river in his first summer or possibly stay in salt water for between one and four years, waxing fat on the abundant food supplies that the ocean provides. Again, as in all of us, sooner or later the urge to reproduce will not be denied.

Returning to the river of his birth from the fleshpots and fine restaurants of 'ocean city' he appears a fine silver-scaled gentleman of one to four pounds in weight, fighting fit, deodorant under his fin pits and ready for love. It was then, and still is, my pleasure to be standing on a convenient rock or wading up to my knees in the blackest water of a dark night with time lapping at my ankles and a handful of split cane or carbon fibre, waiting for him.

Of course hill farming is a profession or vocation that takes most of the daylight hours, and leaves little time for hobbies or any other way of dealing with the trash and stressful residue that remains like a tide mark around the edge of the mind after a day of dealing with complaining argumentative and greedy humanity. Enter again the wonderful sea trout.

Out of respect for the working fisherman, who is usually short of time, he dines very late. In the area of 'the Well Watered Land' his table is spread well after dark, and usually just before or just after midnight. I think I would be honest in saying that there is no greater thrill or relaxation than standing on, in, or by a wide dark river at midnight, watching the tiny silver ripples, 'Watkins-Pitchford-esque' flashing for one instant (a reference to the work of natural history writer and illustrator 'BB' [1905–90]) and then being swallowed up in the dark bosom of the pool.

Imagine if you will the soft swish of the fly line as it explores the night behind you and the pool in front, the complete concentration that is needed to remember the exact distance of the overhanging branches on the far bank and the ever-crowding shrubbery behind. And eventually, and only occasionally, if you are lucky, the sudden swift pull of a take. Even after many years of night fishing my heart still pounds and my mouth goes dry at the feel of a big fish. A firm flick of the wrist to set the hook and then all hell breaks loose.

There is usually a first furious race across or up and down the pool, followed by some serious aerobatics and tail walking, head shaking, tail slapping and short lunatic charges towards tree stumps, sunken bushes, sharp rocks or any of the hundred or so aids to escape that can be found at the bottom of a black river on a dark night. Dartmoor comes to itself after dark: that is its best time. I also come to life after dark: that is my best time. When most of urban humanity has gone home to their warm nests and central heating, the old river soothes with its quiet conversation, the monotonous cries of the screech owls, themselves punctuated by the occasional scream of a vixen in love. The sounds of a Dartmoor night always land well on the ear, with sometimes the boil and roll of a restless fish punctuating the tranquillity for which we all search at various times through our lives.

In general I have no problem with killing as I usually cook and eat everything that I kill, except perhaps a stinking old fox. We have of course been hunters and hunter-gatherers for many thousands of years. For 100,000 generations we have relied as a species on these skills to survive. We are after all only a couple of generations in front of the Inuit, the aboriginals, and the other so-called primitive peoples, and I doubt that two or three generations of comfortable living and woolly liberal thinking will entirely eradicate the instinct for hunting, killing, protecting and providing for one's dependents. Life is always on a knife-edge and we must always keep our survival skills within easy reach. That primeval instinct is always with us; we are merely animals under a light veneer. If we are hungry enough we will eat each other, if we are angry or frightened enough we will kill each other. That knife-edge is always there and it takes very little to push us over it. Our diet has always been partly protein, and most of that protein has come from meat.

Ask any vegetarian why they don't eat meat and the answer is usually: 'I love animals.' Love is a very strong and emotive word. I am very fond of my dog and would rather spend an hour in her company than almost anyone I know and she, of course, is very fond of me; but I would suggest that is merely because I am her pack leader. I suspect that the moment I show any weakness, or someone else comes along with a more interesting hobby or a tastier tin of meat, her loyalties would probably be easily divided.

With animals of course there is always a strict pecking order and the higher up the order you are, the more likely you are to live. Nature is 'red in tooth and claw', and although we would all like to be anthropomorphic and think that our animals love us because they wag their tails or purr and show some sign of recognition, I guess we ought to come to terms with the fact that unfortunately almost all domesticated animals are originally herd or pack animals, and most of their behaviour boils down to dominance, subservience or just plain convenience, much the same as our own species. But I suppose we will always believe that we 'love' them just the same.

RACING TO ORDERS

There was, I suppose, still some racing ambition latent within me. By this time in my life I had run Gilded Gamble in a few point-to-points, the main advantage being her extravagant jump. I had schooled her slowly and carefully and I rode her into the frame a couple of times against some very good opposition. Now I felt the time had come to try for a big one. Never being high on self-confidence I asked Darkie if he would ride on the day.

The word got around that we were trying and half the village decided to go to the races, including all the regulars from the local pub, the Tavistock Inn. The weather was kind to us: it rained heavily for most of the week before the race. When we got onto the course her original starting price was 16 to 1. After her entourage had laid their money down the price had dropped sharply to 4 to 1. Darkie was buoyant and overconfident, I was stressed and felt responsibility for the whole damned village. I took Darkie into the changing tent and laid our strategy on the line very firmly. I explained that the mare was young and would quickly lose concentration, and the key was to keep her covered in midfield for most of the race, and if he was in with a shout he should only come to the front after the last fence.

Four fences from home the silly bugger was twenty lengths in the lead, waving his whip, looking over his shoulder and singing 'Darkie's on a winner!' Coming to the last the mare lost concentration and started looking for her friends – and the rest is history. She pecked at the last and sent 'himself' into the mud where he belonged. I think he found the camouflage useful as a battalion of Tavistock Inn regulars were out for his hide. They had stood to win at least £1000 that day, and in those days that was a useful amount of money.

Jez on Gilded Gamble, Ottery St Mary Point-to-Point, 1970s: 'The best horse I ever had'
PHOTOGRAPH © MARCUS BATH

We still see each other occasionally at a point-to-point or the races and fortunately we have remained friends! The knowledge that some of the horses that had been left so many lengths behind in an 'almost' three-mile point-to-point had themselves gone on to win hunter chases and other races in the National Hunt card boosted my confidence and my ambition to the extent that I settled on the audacious plan of running her at the Cheltenham Festival. I had by this time obtained a provisional trainer's permit.

Cheltenham is an undulating course. It has a long pull up to the finish and I felt that if only the going was heavy, we might even stand a chance of finishing respectably. Cheltenham in the week of the National Hunt Festival is for the amateur quite an awesome goal, and I think it was probably only my youth and naïveté that carried me through. It is in every sense of the word a big course, and the fences are even bigger. Possibly, next to Aintree, they are as big as they come. Many was the long night that I lay awake wondering why the hell I had made that decision. Resources were fairly limited and the mare was very novice, nevertheless we soldiered on with a strict training regime and built the fences a little higher.

We encountered a few minor problems with our training. One fairly puzzling problem was her wind. As she got fitter and into faster work she was very 'stuffy'. Try as we might, we could find no reason for it. The hay was clean and dust free, and she had spent weeks hill trotting on the road, which is the best exercise for respiratory improvement. In fact one of my usual routes for fast trotting involved starting at New Bridge below Poundsgate and trotting back to the top of Sherrill Hill, a distance of some three miles hard climbing.

I remember on one occasion an old Land Rover and loaded horse trailer was grinding its way up New Bridge Hill and we trotted past him. The sight of his face as he saw a horse's head draw level with his window kept me chuckling for the rest of the day.

Generally there was a shine on Gamble's coat and she was feeling well in herself, so well in fact that when I threw a leg over her in the mornings she would let loose with a couple of good bucks, but she was still seriously short in the oxygen department. We ran through all the usual problems and remedies: dusty feed, dusty straw bedding and so on. I eventually came to the conclusion that she was eating her bedding, but she wouldn't eat it while we were looking which made it difficult to prove. So in desperation one night I boxed clever and waited until after dark, in fact until nearly midnight, and shone a strong torch through the box window. Lo and behold, after she thought we had gone she started stuffing straw down her neck as fast as she could. She had obviously realised it was a crime and thought it best to wait until she was alone. Haven't we all felt like that on occasion, especially when suffering from hard exercise and a strict diet? The straw was good quality wheat straw and I have heard trainers say that to eat wheat straw does no harm, but it certainly had a significant effect on her respiratory system. So away went the straw.

Next we thought we would try shredded newspaper: this was only partially successful. Gamble politely refused the bulk of the newspaper but took a liking to the shredded pink parts of the *Financial Times*. Apart from not wanting to encourage her intellectual leanings, we had an outside manure heap and when the shredded paper dried out, in a good stiff breeze you can imagine the bloody mess around the yard and nearby paddocks. There was nothing for it but to go back to wheat straw with a muzzle! But she wasn't going to be beaten. The muzzle had holes at the bottom of it and she spent many happy hours in the dark watches of the night trying to aim the little holes over single stalks of straw and suck. That sort of single-minded tenacity is obviously a plus in the racing field but not much use in the box.

As is usual in racing there were other hiccups on the way to the great festival. One particular problem was a little more humiliating than most. We had decided to run her for practice in a novice handicap 'chase at Newton Abbot. It is a small and fairly slow local track, known amongst the locals in the old days as a 'flapping track', and we thought it would be a useful pipe-opener for Cheltenham. The horse was fit and well handicapped, and we thought we were in with a chance of a place. Just as a final touch, I rang my farrier who lived between us and Newton Abbot and asked him if he could put up a set of aluminium racing plates for the day.

The day dawned fair and promising and we loaded the old girl up into the trailer and set off for the farrier. He was a racing man himself and ushered us in for a cup of tea with his wife while he plated the mare. Either he had a bet on a horse in the same race or he had merely run out of plating nails; either way he put up the plates with shoeing nails which have much larger heads. When we got into the collecting ring, which was in those days a tarmac strip, the old girl looked as if she was walking on stilts. We were immediately called into the stewards' room, given a very stern lecture on bad shoeing practice and fined £50. The embarrassing upshot was that I had to spend ten minutes in the paddock wearing my best Oxfam suit, rasping down the heads of the nails with a rasp swiftly borrowed from the course farrier while the start of the race was held up and hundreds of eyes were turned in my direction. Needless to say there wasn't a queue to buy me a drink in the owners' and members' bar. Anyway the mare performed quite creditably and set us up with high hopes for the festival.

As the great day grew ever closer every waking minute of every day (and most of every night) were taken up with the final preparations concerning training and diet, no *Financial Times*, no straw sucking, just hard sweat and grind except the last two or three days when the hard work slackened off and we just concentrated on a little fast work.

We had decided to enter her in the amateur riders' race on Wednesday 13 March 1985. Everyone was up bright and early and there was a good feel about the whole proceedings. We fuelled up the old Land Rover and hitched up the trailer, checking all the little things that go together with a day racing: bandages, water buckets, various and complicated paraphernalia, not forgetting the colours. Our colours were quite simply black with a red hoop and a black and red hooped silk.

Of course the wise ones among us had to put forward the theory that the mixture of black and red was a considerably bad omen, because the red hoop obviously stood for blood and the black could stand for nothing better than death. Be that as it may, we went chugging up the dual carriageway towards Cheltenham. (Although we were heading for the greatest festival of National Hunt racing in the world, with our elderly Land Rover and horsebox we probably looked like a family of roaming gypsies.) We allowed ourselves an extra hour for emergencies, and although our nerves were jangling we made good time for most of the way until about two miles out of Cheltenham I glanced in the rear view mirror and noticed to my horror a cloud of black smoke emanating from one of the horsebox wheels. The wheel bearing was shot! And of course in those far-off days horseboxes didn't carry spare wheels. By this time there was only about half an hour between us and ignominious failure. I climbed out and kicked it, which didn't improve my toe, the wheel or my temper. No mobile phones then for quick rescue.

There was nothing for it but to run up and down the road searching vainly for a garage. But the gods of racing were with me. Around the next corner I spied an elderly caravan nestling in a bed of stinging nettles. After frantically thrashing the stinging nettles with a stick (which did improve my temper) I discovered that the wheel and axle appeared to be roughly the same size as that of the horse trailer. I quickly composed of small prayer of apology to the god of stinging nettles and summoned up enough courage to knock on the back door of the house. The door was eventually opened by an equally elderly gentleman smoking a pipe. Peering through the cloud of fragrant tobacco smoke, I explained the situation. The old boy was obviously settling down to watch the Cheltenham races on the television which gave me a well-handicapped start. Firmly grasping a situation that required no particular effort from himself, he assured me that if I had time to take the bearing from the caravan axle, and if it fitted, I was welcome to it: I could have kissed him, pipe and all.

At least I was honest enough to assure him that we did not stand much of a chance but were there for the experience. I slipped him the race and number – it seemed only fair!

We rolled onto the course with very few minutes to spare. The crowd was massive and there were enough helicopters to make a passable wasps' nest, along with the biggest campsite you could imagine. I don't think I've ever seen so many happy Irishmen in my life. Many of them were from the more rural backwoods areas, flashing large wads of badly folded money – I almost felt at home! This time I didn't have to demean myself in front of the crowd around the paddock, although I felt the Irish would probably have understood, particularly after the 200,000 pints of Guinness that they had over the festival. The mare was feeling well and the going suited her. For this occasion I had given the leg up to a lady jockey, Janine Mills. Janine was experienced and had good horses of her own.

The horses all cantered quietly down to the start, in complete obedience to Mr Starter and circled quietly while the starter's assistant checked girths and surcingles. They all came up quietly into line including Gilded Gamble (much to my relief) and they were off! The first jump on a steeplechase course is usually wide and easy and the mare took it in style, making up half a length on everyone else. By this stage my stomach was churning and my vision was blurred. I was always much more comfortable riding in a race than watching a horse of mine under another pilot.

It is always an amazing advantage if a horse is well schooled over steeplechase and hunting fences before going on to National Hunt racing. Each fence that is taken well and not fiddled can gain a horse half a length and, with experience, both horse and jockey will gradually learn to get their stride pattern in order well before the fence. Of course in a steeplechase with seventeen or nineteen fences, this represents quite an advantage.

For most of the first circuit she held her own and what she lacked in speed she made up for in jumping ability, and considering her opposition were all in a far better class than she was used to, she held her own rather well. When on the final circuit she came up that long hill towards the finish, she proved her staying power and gained two or three places much to our delight. We left Cheltenham that day with a sound horse and a glow of satisfaction.

Incidentally the wheel bearing held up for the journey home. It's nice to have a little luck on race days. In those days I don't think it was possible to buy a television recording of a race, but I suppose I could honestly say that it was one of the most exciting days of my life, and old Gamble and I went on to have many more wonderful adventures.

THE WIND OF CHANGE

*'The hobnailed boot that had previously carried
the knowledge, care, experience and instinct of the
moorland way of life has been replaced by the rubber
walking boot, forcing the "right to roam" on most of
the open countryside…'*

...SNAPS AT THE HEELS OF EXPERIENCE

Alongside all the pleasant racing adventures, my real bread and butter was obviously farming. I have in all my life been lucky enough to make a living out of a job that I love; I guess perhaps 'vocation' would be more appropriate than job. There are very few things more satisfying in life than the smell of newly ploughed earth or newly mown grass, or the thrill of helping a calf or a lamb take its first milk from its mother. There are of course the silly and the thick that can't or won't really work out that the tits are attached to the blunt end of a cow or a sheep and not the sharp end. Sometimes at 3am on a cold and wet night when you are battling with temperature, stress and tiredness, the automatic care gene with which we are all endowed boils over into temporary hatred for the little bugger and you could cheerfully strangle it and save both you and its mother a job. But of course when the warm sticky milk suddenly hits the spot and a new life is kindled to take its place in the old world, the butting head and ridiculously wagging tail signals a new joy and peace for all three of us, and the top of Dartmoor on a bleak windy night is once more a good place to be.

It was at about this time of my life and career that I felt a wind of change blowing over Dartmoor, a wind that was destined to threaten its very existence as an attractive and treasured man-made entity; a political wind driven by greed, envy and prejudice.

Personally I was never a natural politician, partly because I was not comfortable with the idea that I had the right to tell anyone else what to do, and mostly because no one would listen to me if I did. Even so I decided it might be a good idea as an indigenous Dartmoor farmer to put myself up for the foremanship of the local Commoners' Association, if only to keep my finger on the pulse, so to speak. Our old friend Peter Hannaford had been the Foreman of Spitchwick Common for over thirty years; in fact if my memory serves me it was somewhere around thirty-six years. We have on Spitchwick one of the oldest manorial Court Leets in the country consisting of Foreman, Reeve, Pound-Keeper, Ale-Taster and Tithing-Man, and of course the Lord of the Manor and his agent.

This collection of worthies holds sway over the association's meetings and criticisms, when hopefully constructive suggestions from the floor are dealt with, the floor consisting of the rest of the commoners and cottagers. Anyway, I was voted on as Foreman somewhere around the year of HM The Queen's Silver Jubilee in 1977.

On the slopes of Yar Tor

As Foreman of Spitchwick Common I was automatically entitled to become a member of the then Dartmoor Commoners' Association. The chairman of the association in those days was Herbert Whitley. Herbert was a good chairman, a wise counsellor and had influence and an ear in Westminster. It was early political days for Dartmoor, but even then we as an association felt a strong insidious and developing encroachment from many other bodies that claimed an interest in the management of Dartmoor.

It might have been selfish of us, but we all felt very strongly that Dartmoor was under threat and that the Dartmoor that we and our forefathers as agriculturalists had created over many thousands of years was in imminent danger of being submerged and lost forever under the increasing clamour for authoritative representation by 'bandwagon bodies' with a little knowledge. Many of these bodies were governed by a complete self-interest, with a very few that had more noble motives; but none of them, or the general public's unelected representatives, had the knowledge or experience to preserve the visual aspect of Dartmoor that farming, warrening and tin mining had created. Nor indeed had they the knowledge or experience to farm, husband or control the livestock that have always been the necessary tools of preservation on the moor. After all, it has always been the many feet and teeth, bovine, equine and ovine, which have created the visual aspect of Dartmoor that is so cherished by everyone today.

In the first half of the last century, many thousands of cattle and sheep were herded up onto the Forest, travelling the old driftways running from Kingsbridge, the South Hams and surrounding areas to summer on the high moor; and apart from the summer visitors, there were at least 30,000 ponies grazing the high plateau throughout the whole year. It was inconceivable that a collection of a young 'wet behind the ears' students, fresh from college and now working for DEFRA and English Nature, could appreciate or understand the toil and sometime heartbreak that, combined with generations of experience, was essential to manage the Dartmoor livestock and in turn the flora and fauna of the commons.

So it was then, under the guidance of Herbert Whitley, that we abandoned the old Dartmoor Commoners' Association and created a Dartmoor Commoners' Council with a view to placing a Bill before Parliament to be known as the Dartmoor Commons Bill. The council would consist of sixteen Dartmoor farmers and commoners, two landowners, one representative of the Duchy of Cornwall and two members nominated by the National Park Authority, up to a maximum of twenty-eight members.

Under the terms of the new Bill the Commoners' Council itself, having regard to conservation and the enhancement of the natural beauty of the Commons, was responsible for all the agricultural aspects of the Commons of Dartmoor including the burning of heather, grass, gorse and bracken to such an extent as in their opinion was desirable for the purposes of livestock husbandry; also to ensure that the Commons were not overstocked, and for that purpose the council was to fix the number of animals of any description that may be dispastured on the commons.

This left the Dartmoor National Park authority as representatives of national government with the frankly unenviable task of making bylaws to control the general public and to supervise access, planning applications and so on. It was so simple! Or at least should have been. Two separate authorities working side-by-side would take responsibility for and make laws to control those aspects of the National Park that fell within their remit and experience.

We were fortunate enough to enlist the help of our local MP, Antony Steen (yes, him with the big house and the jealousy complex) who presented our Bill to the office of the Clerk of the Parliaments (House of Lords) and the Private Bill office of the House of Commons (all terribly important stuff). But at least the Bill was eventually passed and entered into the laws of the country.

After all the work, stress and worry we could read in triumph Part 3 of the Bill that stated under regulation of common rights by the Commoners' Council (and I quote) 'it shall be the duty of Commoners' Council to take such steps as appear to be necessary and reasonably practical for the maintenance of the Commons and the promotion of proper standards of livestock husbandry thereon'. What a wonderful regulation for us to savour! In our naïveté we truly believed that we had protected the past and secured the future, at least for our lifetimes and hopefully our children's. How wrong we were!

Now I sit here, thirty years later, to see that the Commoners' Council, contrary to the perceived necessity of its existence, has been emasculated to the extent that the few remaining decisions it is allowed to make are mainly concerned with the colour painted on a sheep's backside or the amount of 'clear days' wherein sheep have to be removed from the common. Momentous and earth-shattering decisions!

The statutory powers, by which the important regulations and decisions on all the agricultural aspects of the Commons of Dartmoor are made, have been removed from the commoners and their elected representatives and replaced by a series of grants and subsidies allegedly paid to farmers to enhance traditional maintenance and conservation. These are actually a method of blackmailing the farmers (who can ill-afford to lose the money) into accepting ill-thought-out and badly conceived methods of so-called conservation, which have substantially altered the flora and fauna of the moor, also its visual aspect, leaving it overgrown and understocked with no thought for sustainable agricultural practice or tradition. We might as well have accepted a handful of coloured beads!

Where there were grazing animals and a peaceful, pastoral and traditional agriculture, there are now chainsaws and brush cutters. Where there were ground-nesting birds on the open moor there are now spaniels and labradoodles!

The hobnailed boot that had previously carried the knowledge, care, experience and instinct of the moorland way of life has been replaced by the rubber walking boot, forcing the 'right to roam' on most of the open countryside. Even the quiet rural footpath that local children used to walk to school, or the Sunday morning family to church, is now pitted and rutted every week, or even every day, by hundreds of heavy walking boots and mountain bikes. The heavy brush and overgrowth itself is forcing both people and animals to overuse the paths and tracks while DEFRA, basking in its paternalistic authoritarian naïveté, seems to feel that it is a class apart and the only body that has the preservation and stewardship of the countryside at heart, while the farmers and countrymen are obviously hell-bent on destroying it!

I don't recall seeing any of them in the rain, sleet or mud post-5pm or on weekends, holidays or bank holidays. If it can't be done in a centrally heated forty-hour week it won't be done at all. If generations of Dartmoor farmers had taken that attitude and opted for an easy life on a public salary, Dartmoor would not be Dartmoor! But I suppose soapboxes even on firm moral ground will only hold us marginally above the threshold of boredom. So out of respect for the reader's patience I will move on to the embryonic realisation that was slowly developing in my mind, that working an eighty-hour week on a couple of hundred acres was not going to be enough to pay the bills, as it had in Father's and Grandfather's day.

TALES FROM THE SADDLE

The idea adopted after the last Great War by the 'land of the rising sun' appealed to me, namely: 'Look around, find a successful business, study it carefully, copy it and try to improve on it.'

To this end I started to take tentative steps towards the leisure industry to subsidise my farming activities – it only seems like yesterday but it must have been over thirty years ago. So combining my love of horses with my equal love of Dartmoor and my surroundings, I decided to study one or two of the more successful riding establishments in the West of England. We studied, we copied and very occasionally, and very gradually, we succeeded in subsidising the farm and the cattle. At first it was obviously a joy to work with horses and give a great many people the pleasure of experiencing the sights, sounds and scents of Dartmoor from the elevated position of a horse, with the added advantage that they did not have to look where they were putting their feet!

The stories, experiences and occasionally downright terror gifted to us free and gratis by the great British public would fill a book on their own (and there was always the slight advantage that the customers were a captive audience and could not stray into danger, climb fences, gates and so on). In general it was a reasonable assumption that you could keep them from damaging the environment or themselves, or perambulate into the paths of wrongfulness thereby antagonising the local peasantry. My new family – Tracey, Katie and I – fall into fits of laughter when looking back.

I remember many years ago one particular customer who probably supplied us with the complete range of emotions, from quiet concern to helpless laughter. She was a retired nightclub singer who had travelled the country singing at various venues including, I believe, the old jail club at Bodmin in Cornwall. In middle age she was still attractive and took very great care of her appearance, insisting on wearing (while riding) a range of interesting wigs and hairpieces. Her natural hair had probably not seen daylight for many years and consequently had grown very sparse and thin. Her major nightmare was being seen minus either make-up or wig. She flatly refused to wear a safety hat and had roped the newest headpiece down with a good colourful headscarf: 'Anything that the Queen can get away with, so can I!'

She was a novice rider and not particularly bold, and it so happened one day that returning from quite a long ride (which Tracey, my new wife, and I were escorting) we were suddenly serenaded by an ear-piercing scream from the middle of the ride. So like 'Joris and He' en route from Ghent, we spun round and spurred hastily to the scene, expecting at any moment to find carnage and or corpses.

The scene was more dreadful than that. The good lady's headscarf had been removed as it was rubbing her neck and a teenage blackthorn bush with high spirits and malign intent had reached down and plucked the latest expensive wig from her head! The poor dear was not quite agile enough to dismount and grab the wig, as the bush had deposited it in mud directly behind her horse. It was a narrow path and the horse immediately behind her had added to the fun by uttering a terrified snort and striking out at the horrible hairy thing in front of it with a forefoot. Multitasking to a fine point, it then deposited its rider in a gorse bush. No one could stop laughing, while the poor soul sat with hands on head and wailed. It was as good as a play and, if anything, it got better.

We finished the ride and at home had sat the victim down with a nice cup of tea. Thinking to placate her injured pride, we then offered to run the wig through the washing machine, which we duly did, then hung it on the washing line to dry. Halfway through the second cup of tea and a nice wholemeal biscuit, the slowly returning peace was shattered by a fusillade of barking and growling from the garden. The farm dogs had discovered the same hairy beast perched menacingly on Mother's washing line and, to the accompaniment of more helpless laughter, with bottlebrush tails, hackles up and eyes out on stalks they were giving it their all. The lady hastily retired to her boudoir.

On another occasion we were trekking round the tops of the tors, trying to find both a breeze and a view. There were ten or a dozen horses and ponies on the ride, the sun beat down out of a copper sky and each horse's head had a halo of insects of both the biting and just the bloody irritating kind. We had managed to find the view but not the breeze, and we decided to come down off the tops through the heavy fern which was all of three feet high (and some places six) to the valley below.

At the back of the ride we had a 15-hand palomino mare called Pinkie. Now Pinkie was as steady as a rock, a good money earner and, as far as we knew to that date, afraid of nothing on earth. We had just exchanged pleasantries with a family on the tor before descending and everything was progressing smoothly when approximately halfway down Pinkie, suddenly laying her ears back and gritting her teeth, bolted down through the ferns galloping hell for leather. She unseated nearly every rider in the string, depositing her own en route.

Wondering what the hell had got into her I swung my horse in front in a vain effort to stop her progress. She sidestepped me like an international scrum-half and – still looking serious and determined – bolted out of the ferns into the grassy valley below, at which point all was revealed. The family we had spoken to on top of the tor had with them a pet Staffordshire terrier. It was no longer with them: it was attached to Pinkie's tail and had obviously been invisible to all concerned for the last quarter of a mile. Pinkie was a contemplative soul with an elephantine memory, and for the rest of her long life, if she met anything less than two feet in height and coloured brindle, she made a point of biting it.

We had many adventures with Pinkie. On one occasion we were returning from a hunt. I was driving in front with a four-horsebox while Pinkie and her special friend

Jasper, who was Tracey's horse, were following close behind in a horse trailer, pulled by a four-wheel-drive. The driver was a young graduate from the local agricultural college with unfortunately not much experience of driving a horse trailer. The horses moved slightly and the trailer started to snake. The lad hit the brakes with the inevitable result that both trailer and vehicle turned over in the road. It must have been at least a quarter of a mile before I realised that they were no longer in my mirrors. We turned around and went back to find a dazed and badly frightened driver, everything upside down, with two horses lying one on top of the other. Pinkie, God bless her, was lying underneath, very still and quiet, presumably dead, while Jasper on top of her was thrashing and kicking at the door of the trailer which was bent and buckled and impossible to open. It was an awful moment for all concerned.

The emergency services arrived very quickly and set up floodlights and pneumatic cutting gear which they used very effectively to open up the trailer like a tin can. We dragged Jasper out. Unfortunately he had kicked and struggled to the front of the box, bending his neck back and breaking it. Once he was clear we went back to remove Pinkie's carcass, but as I was attaching the chain to her hind feet I noticed her very cautiously open one eye. Through a veil of tears I patted her on the neck, whereupon the old cow opened both eyes, jumped to her feet, walked out onto the verge and started grazing as if blue flashing lights, sirens and fire engines were an everyday occurrence. My veil of tears turned into a flood and I was joined unfortunately by my poor wife who had more to cry about than I.

One of Pinkie's many claims to fame was teaching a fourteen-year-old novice rider called Philip Collington. Philip learned his trade on Pinkie and went on to be a useful jockey under rules, eventually becoming champion Arab racing jockey and spending a very successful and probably lucrative time in Dubai.

Over the many years of escorting customers around Dartmoor we collected almost as many strange and eccentric horses as we had strange and eccentric riders to place upon them. Once we bought a couple of horses from Eastern Europe (I think it was Poland). We sold one of them to a small gay chap call Steve who promptly named the horse Jason. Apparently the poor sweet thing was at that time in love with Jason Donovan (no accounting for taste!). Jason was a black with some white markings, particularly around his fetlocks where he had been hobbled as a youngster. The horse was, in local terminology, 'as hard as a black pig' with a mule-like constitution and manners to match. It proved impossible to teach him, reason with him or actually do anything with him apart from working him hard, which he seemed to appreciate, but Steve loved him (I suppose somebody had to).

Steve frequently brought his middle-aged partner to see the horse. They always used to ask if they could camp on the farm overnight. Oddly enough they usually insisted on having a sloping field in which to pitch their tent. Although our stable girls always had vivid imaginations I don't think anyone ever quite worked out the reason, or had nerve enough to ask.

One of our other 'larger than life' horse characters was Freckles (now sadly departed). A placid rotund white grey, she plodded through the years earning her keep and not really asking anything of anyone, but Freckles was living proof of how the inexperienced horseman – or more to the point the very experienced horseman – can still occasionally come unstuck. The old girl was bombproof to the point of boredom and there was nothing exciting in her life for 364 days a year, but on the 365th day she did 'go to the ball!'

Every year on the second Tuesday in September Freckles was deposited at Widecombe-in-the-Moor to spend the day acting the part of the famous old grey mare of 'Tom Cobley' fame. Widecombe Fair is one of the more famous fairs in the West Country and it is attended by thousands of people. All day Freckles plodded through the crowds carrying Uncle Tom and enjoying the occasional ice cream or half pint of cider, standing under the tannoy, being molested by small children, sworn at by even smaller dogs, dodging cars, charabancs and steam engines (with which she thought she had a certain amount in common) and through the whole hot, sweaty, turgid and incredibly noisy day showed never a sign of alarm or complaint.

But back at home in her own comfort zone she had one particular terror. If you were grooming her with a stiff dandy brush or a curry comb, when cleaning the brush you must take the little ball of grey hair firmly in your hand and place it in the bin. If accidentally you dropped it on the floor around her feet and if perchance there was enough breeze to roll the ball of hair a few inches along the ground, Freckles immediately went berserk. She would plunge in her headcollar like a salmon on a line, scatter or injure anyone within range of her thrashing hooves and if successful in breaking her rope, would bolt out of the yard

Freckles 'in her element' at Widecombe Fair, 2012: 'One of the best-known horses on Dartmoor'

with a speed that – given her portly figure – one would not have believed possible.

Her antics just went to prove that however experienced or capable you are, when dealing with a herd animal that has survived for millions of years by being suspicious and fleet of foot, one can never be too careful, and however careful you may be it is never possible to forestall all emergencies.

I remember once taking out a particularly difficult ride of novices. It was a beautiful day and halfway round we had to pass a perfectly innocent and innocuous-looking car parked under a tree on the side of the road. As the car was obviously empty and we had no equine autophobes amongst us I allowed them all to carry on past the car. As the ride came alongside, a small but ferocious canine vacated the footwell and hit the window like a bullet accompanied by a shrill scream of wrath. Needless to say, our passive prey animals scattered in all directions depositing bodies at every point of the compass.

I cursed myself for not being experienced enough, after forty years, to realise that a car parked in the shade of a tree could possibly hold a small bad-tempered dog, but that is the sort of anticipation that is needed when dealing with horses and trying to keep customers alive.

SOME CELEBS

We have also over the years had some strange and eccentric celebs, with almost as much character as the horses. One interesting afternoon we had the pleasure of the company of Chay Blyth, who decided to grace us with the company of both himself and his large fat grey cob. We had been travelling up the East Dart river on the eastern bank heading for its confluence with the Wallabrook, at which point we had to cross over and gain the west side of the latter. By the time we got to the meeting of the waters, Mr Blyth had forged ahead by fifty yards or more and was still doing a good twenty knots. Sensing that he was in imminent danger of getting lost, I called out very politely to ask him to come back and join the ride. Whether it was the wind in his sails or just the sound of the river in his ears I know not, but suffice it to say he took quite a long time to tack back and join us, and when he did his face was a slightly different colour than it had been upon his leaving; and as the recipient of my merry quip about being able to find his way around the oceans of the world but having difficulty crossing the Wallabrook, it gained an even deeper hue.

Another strange character that provided us with much amusement was the singer Sinead O'Connor. She arrived in the middle of Dartmoor plus entourage with the avowed intent of making a film 'The Maid of Orleans'. The particular piece of truth-stretching that involved us was a take where Joan of Arc, dressed in full battle armour and brandishing a broadsword, bore down upon her enemies at full gallop screaming like a banshee and putting the fear of God into them.

Diminutive and bald she might have been, but she managed to put the fear of God into me (a restless and confused Irish soul if ever I saw one). The general scenario was reasonable but for the fact that she could not ride, which in the short term negated any possibility of her galloping downhill for any purpose. After much coffee housing, 'luvvie-ing' and discussion, it was decided that with a little tuition plus a close and proactive accompaniment by me on a steady hunter, she might manage to gallop uphill. To this end we all adjourned to Bellever Tor, magnificent in its benign tranquillity. In those days there was a nice gentle grassy track leading up to the tor.

Babeny clapper bridge, on the Wallabrook – 'my favourite bridge'

The plan was that I should gallop beside her holding her reins and peel off immediately pre-camera, leaving her to do her fearsome bit. All went well up to a point; but armour is heavy and helmets have next to no vision, added to which I was stressed and thespians don't generally float my boat. The result was that during the frantic preparation for the take, none of us had noticed that the Tavistock Geriatric Club had wandered onto the grassy track and set up a beautiful picnic with a view to a nice lunch while they watched the fun.

Concentrating as I was on keeping Madame in the plate I wound her up to a full thundering gallop and peeled off without bothering to look very far ahead.

I am not sure to this day whether the visor of her helmet had fallen over her eyes or whether the red mist of battle gifted by long-dead Celtic ancestors had come upon her; either way the effect was much the same. It really is amazing how fast older pensioners can scuttle when the need arises. One can only hope that the majority of them were not claiming disability benefit, for if any of the film clips ever arrived in the public domain they would most surely have been done for fraud. The only casualties were two old dears who leaped backwards and were found, bloomers uppermost in a whortleberry bush, and one retired and dignified gentleman whose back went into spasm halfway up a rowan tree.

On the subject of photographic evidence, I remember we spent one happy day in the company of David Bailey and his wife. Mr Bailey was determined to take some shots of his wife galloping across the top of Dartmoor with her hair flowing beautifully in the breeze. Again, she was not a rider, and the manner of her riding and proposed lack of a safety helmet left some searching questions from the health and safety aspect.

'Filmies', as Ms Peckwitt's (Scottish author Lillian Beckwith) Hebridean friends would describe them, often arrived in chattering flocks on the high moor, as gaudy and quarrelsome as flocks of starlings, bringing with them their own particular style of arrogance and insensitivity. I particularly remember one bunch that landed at the farm. They were trying to produce a very expensive film about the American Revolution and they were particularly keen on filming some shots of an American backwoodsman being pursued by a pack of dogs. Being rather short of 'coon-hounds' in our particular neck of the backwoods they had hit upon the idea of using a pack of foxhounds or similar.

They had approached the Masters of Foxhounds Association, which fortunately included a couple of packs of bloodhounds amongst its membership. Somewhere in the small print of the MFH rulebook there must have been a clause prohibiting any connection with 'filmies, tinkers or other itinerants'. Fortunately, it so happened that at that time we had a friend, Mr Body, whose particular pastime was owning and hunting a pack of bloodhounds. He kindly suggested that I should be promoted to acting huntsman, and pursue the backwoodsman for the benefit of the film and the not insignificant amount of cash that would accompany the hiring of three horses and a pack of hounds.

The day of filming dawned and we arose at 'sparrows-fart' to transport both horses and hounds over to the other side of the moor. On early arrival at Burrator Reservoir, the appointed venue for the shoot, I was ushered into a wardrobe tent and cocooned in an outfit that proclaimed me to be a cross between an English gentleman-squire and a Captain of the Dragoon Guards. From there I was escorted to the make-up tent and anointed with greasepaint and dubious advice as in how to ride my horse and talk to the 'doggies'.

At this juncture I was becoming 'rustically-uncomfortable'. The final curtain came when a small person with a face like a fish strutted into the tent and eyed me coldly. I might add that at this stage of my life I wore a small goatee beard which he grasped between finger and thumb and tweaked! With the firm instruction to 'take that off or you don't work, luvvie', I didn't feel at all luvvie, in fact rather closer to murderous. So mumbling into my £1000 beard I stalked out, to be followed by the comment: 'If you won't do it, luvvie, leave the horses and we'll do it our bloody selves'!

'Home, James and don't spare the horses!'

'I FEAR ONE HAS RUN OVER ONE'S GOOSE'

Going back a few years, I can recall that the day the landlord started murdering his tenant's stock was an eventful day in many respects. We had been informed at the last moment, as is normal for security purposes, that 'His Nibs' was to grace Babeny and its tenants with a royal visit. This of course involved some last-minute preparation (as in another visit to Oxfam for me and to a hairdresser for the wife).

Fortunately we were blissfully unaware of the protocol and security that was involved in such an honour, and although we made ourselves as presentable as the normal routine of Dartmoor farming would allow, we were slightly taken aback by the very early arrival of three RIVs (Rapid Intervention Vehicles) which appeared to be customised Range Rovers equipped with darkened bullet-proof glass and a gaggle of very smart and very large gentlemen, not forgetting one large and very smart lady who demanded to use the lavatory.

HRH Prince Charles visits Babeny, July 1978: Mark and Dee Dee presenting him with a model of a Dartmoor longhouse they helped their grandmother Freda to make

In my innocence I directed her to the outside convenience. My suggestion was greeted with a strained but patient smile that had 'Rustic idiot' written all over it and a further demand to use the inside lavatory. Having directed her upstairs I was vaguely intrigued to hear the doors of all the bedrooms, all the wardrobes and all the cupboards swiftly opened and closed. Heaven only knows what she must have found under the beds. Whatever it might have been, on her return her smile had a knowing look to it.

Our 'heir apparent' stepped lightly out of his helicopter looking relaxed and cheerful. After all it is his farm and he has been familiar with Dartmoor for decades, having hunted over it and visited various farms on many occasions.

The family and I were lined up for introduction, the only *faux* pas being on my own. I forgot to incline my head while shaking hands, but he didn't seem to notice. Throughout the visit he showed a polite and I believe genuine interest in the farm, in particular the old Dartmoor longhouse that was originally the farmhouse and is now a farm building. The old building, like most old Dartmoor buildings, does not suffer unduly from excessive daylight and as we had no mains electricity at that time, all our lights and gadgets were powered by an elderly diesel generator, a truly wonderful machine made by Lister of Dursley, England, equipped with large half-tonne flywheels and a pre-war character all of its own. But I digress.

The Prince, taking his courteous interest to the limit, decided to enter the building to inspect it and promptly cracked the royal bonce on a low beam. As he staggered back I took to my heels, running out of the doorway intending to hand crank the old generator in order to illuminate the situation and avoid any more injury to the royal person. I don't believe I had sprinted more than three paces from the door when a very large and extremely active royal bodyguard pounced. I was pinned to the ground by a hand the size of a haunch of venison while the other hand hovered around his left breast. Had I been a terrorist with a Kalashnikov he could not have moved quicker or appeared more menacing.

I was told later by an interested neighbour across the valley that during the time of the visit two heavily armed men were doubling it around the boundary hedges in opposite directions.

During the visit we were obliged to smile politely whilst being fed some ill-conceived rubbish about organic farming and indigenous cattle, probably placed in the royal head by a sea-level agricultural student with no bills to pay but good, if naïve, intent. Three or four years ago, for example, the government decided that organically produced food is no better for you than food produced by modern methods. Wow, such common sense in the face of a world food shortage!

Eventually equerries and bodyguards pulled back into their rapid intervention vehicles, presumably with a view to getting to the next stop and checking security before 'himself' arrived. They were unfortunately closely attended by Timothy the gander who, puffed up with paternal pride and enjoying the congratulations and encouragement of his family, charged valiantly at the rear wheel of the swiftly departing vehicle and put his head under it.

The landlord, surveying the scene through a cloud of white feathers from the steps of his helicopter, mumbled something to the effect of, 'one appears to have run over one's goose'! I didn't have the heart to tell him that Timothy was actually a gander, and that both his family and mine would be in need of intensive counselling.

Clarry (1921–2004) and Freda (1923–2015) Wilkinson, Christmas 1993

IN CONCLUSION

THERE COMES A TIME IN THE AFFAIRS OF MAN when he feels that he has achieved many of the things that far-off raw ambition demanded. My life is at last relatively peaceful and hopefully uneventful.

My wife Tracey and I have been together now for over twenty-five years. Our daughter Katie has grown up and left home fully feathered and successfully launched from the home tree into a mad world. My two children Mark and Dee Dee have long since grown up and achieved success in their own particular fields – Dee Dee and her husband Darren now live at Babeny and run the farm and riding stable – and there will always be enough left to do for all of us to take up many lifetimes. In 2016 ambition is just as important as half a century ago.

I am a worrier by nature, but lately I find it increasingly difficult to find something to worry about, or perhaps I am just mellowing with age. Strangely, actions that were once instinctive and careless – making love, killing or dogmatic opinion – nowadays seem to need a little more thought and consideration prior to action.

I still am and always have been fascinated by the old characters that have marched before me through the pages of Dartmoor's history. Through my life I have from time to time suffered an identity crisis; perhaps schizophrenia would be too strong a word, but I have always been a bit of a dreamer, forever trying to place my feet in other men's shoes. The old questions of childhood often bubble to the surface such as: 'Why am I me?' 'What would it have been like to be him?' and so on, and I am always wishing to live two or three lives at the same time. Unfortunately that can never be possible. Perhaps all these things were part and parcel of my dual upbringing? But now in later life, having discovered the joy of the written (if badly spelt) word, the possibilities are endless.

Occasionally I find time to sit under my Rowan tree and watch her narrow leaves like fingers stretching from the branches that point East, West, North and South, perhaps indicating a passage through time both backwards and forwards. The berries of the rowan, like the fruits of life, have only a short season. Her trunk is disfigured now, buffeted by the winds of generations, still sturdy but in places scarred by the teeth of fickle fortune; her ancestors have surveyed the paths of human energy, criss-crossing the moor, tracing the footprints of men who have led lives far more interesting than mine, fine strong characters striding through the years without fear or favour. Would they have allowed us to share their time or thought us fools for trying?

One of her branches points to the northeast to the two-hundred-acre Warren at Soussons, the domain of John Leaman the warrener… but that is a story perhaps best left for another time.

Redundant farm buildings at Laughter Hole

GLOSSARY

ammil   encasing layer of ice on leaves, twigs etc, resulting from
                        falling rain freezing on contact with vegetation etc.

batter   embankment
blackcock   blackgame, black grouse
blasts, fuzz fleeces bundles of gorse
bohereen   narrow lane (Ireland)

clamp   potato 'cave'
clitter   scatter of granite rocks
crib   elevenses

dagging   *see* tail-locking
dimpsey   dusk
dishwasher   pied wagtail
dog fox   male fox

fern ticket   courting licence – 'escorting a young lady off into the
                        ferns on a summer's day… It was always a joke
                        at the youth club!'
flitch   shoulder (pig)
fuzzpig   hedgehog

klickiting time   fox mating time

lackanay   piece of excess material sometimes found in a
                        newborn foal's mouth, dried and used as a charm
lear   home area

mattocks 'twobills' mattock with two blades

penny pies	pennywort
prang	pitchfork
quat	squat, flat
quick-beam	rowan (tree)
reave	vestigial hedge-bank
Saltash-rig	'a wet backside and no fish'
score	20lb
shaver	badger
shinner	members of Sinn Fein (Ireland)
shippon	cow shed
shot iron	gun
stock	hunting tie
strolls, windrows	loose hay
swaling	heather burning
tail-locking	cutting away the dung-matted wool from a sheep's back end
tallet	loft
teddies	potatoes
teddy oggie	pasty
tush	tusk (pig)
vag	section (turf or peat)
wad	section (of hay)
wain	two-wheeled cart
water ouzel	dipper
white throat	weasel